PENGUIN BOOKS

THE BEST OF FLOYD

Keith Floyd was born in 1943 and educated at Wellington School, Somerset. Since then he has devoted his life to cooking, except for a few brief excursions into the army and the antiques and wine trades. He has presented a number of highly successful television cookery series, recently including *Floyd on Africa*, and is the author of several bestselling books, including *Floyd on Oz*, *Floyd on Spain*, *Far Flung Floyd*, *Floyd on Italy*, *Floyd on Africa* and *Floyd on Hangovers*, all of which are published by Penguin. When he is not hurtling around the world he spends his time in southern Ireland.

THE BEST OF
FLOYD
MY GREATEST HITS

KEITH FLOYD

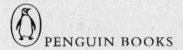
PENGUIN BOOKS

PENGUIN BOOKS

Published by the Penguin Group

Penguin Books Ltd, 27 Wrights Lane, London w8 5TZ, England
Penguin Putnam Inc., 375 Hudson Street, New York, New York 10014, USA
Penguin Books Australia Ltd, Ringwood, Victoria, Australia
Penguin Books Canada Ltd, 10 Alcorn Avenue, Toronto, Ontario, Canada M4V 3B2
Penguin Books (NZ) Ltd, 182–190 Wairau Road, Auckland 10, New Zealand

Penguin Books Ltd, Registered Offices: Hardmondsworth, Middlesex, England

First published by Michael Joseph 1995
Published in Penguin Books 1997
1 3 5 7 9 10 8 6 4 2

Set in 10.5/14pt Monotype Bembo
Typeset by Rowland Phototypesetting Ltd, Bury St Edmunds, Suffolk
Printed in England by Clays Ltd, St Ives plc

CONTENTS

$\mathcal{A}$CKNOWLEDGEMENTS

I would like to thank BBC Books Ltd for permission to reprint selected recipes from the following publications: *Floyd on Fish*, *Floyd on Fire*, *Floyd on France*, *Floyd on Britain and Ireland* and *Floyd's American Pie*; and HarperCollins Publishers Ltd for permission to reproduce selected recipes from *A Feast of Floyd*.

The titles listed below are those in which recipes in *The Best of Floyd* first appeared, followed by the pages on which they can be found in this book:

ＪNTRODUCTION

It was a quiet night in my Bristol restaurant. I was bored waiting for the last couple to leave. I was worried about business. I was tired. It had been a long day and I wanted to go home.

I was sitting sipping a brandy and kicking my legs on the stainless worktop when my waitress announced that 'The gentleman on table three would like to talk to you.' I drained my glass, wiped my face and hands, adjusted my bow-tie and wandered reluctantly over to the table. The table. It was a battle-field strewn with the corpses of lobsters and mussels. Breadcrumbs floated in a lake of spilt wine. A half-extinguished cigarette smouldered on the crumpled paper table cover.

The 'gentleman' was sucking a draught of red wine from a very large glass. He was flushed, smiling and exuberant. 'Dear boy,' he said, 'have a glass.' The bottle was empty.

'I'll have a cognac,' I said.

'So will I,' said he.

The waitress brought the drinks. We chinked glasses and drank.

'So?' I said.

'My name's David,' he said, reaching for the uncorked cognac bottle, 'David Pritchard. And this,' he said, waving vaguely to his female companion, 'is my PA, Frances.'

Frances said, 'Pleased to meet you,' and was not drunk. By the time the bottle was half-empty she had departed. David did not say goodbye. He was munching some cheese, talking, gesticulating and slurping some port. I don't remember how he got the port.

So he said, 'I'm a television producer. For the BBC.' He wore an open-necked shirt, a red communist scarf, jeans and blue trainers. And he continued, 'I've got a Peugeot 304. A blue one. More port? Could I come here and film you? Cooking? It'd only take an hour or so. For my programme, with a rabbit or something that could feed a family for a couple of pounds. Another port?'

'Yes, that's fine,' I said.

He stood up. He is a big man, six foot or more. Knocked over a glass and staggered into the night. Ten years ago. And it was a night that changed my life. For better and for worse.

Before I met Pritchard I was a cook, and a good one. Now? Now I'm a television cook and a food writer, and confused. I am pilloried by the press and entombed in Madame Tussaud's. I earn lots of money and pay lots of lawyers and accountants to tell me that the last lawyer and accountant were no good. People talk to me about food and ask where my wine is. They are surprised when I alight from the train in Paddington without a glass in my hand. People wave at me and smile, and businessmen drink my wine. I can pay my electricity bill and fill the tank of my car and have no problems getting a restaurant table. And this because of Pritchard.

We have eaten and drunk and cooked around the world. In fine kitchens, over a wood fire, in a clay pot, on a boat, on a train or in a field, on gas, on dung, in straw, on charcoal, in the heat, the rain, the wind and the snow. In the desert, in the jungle, on the streets, while people stopped and stared and wondered what that man was doing. And all the time Clive (North) was quietly pointing his camera while Pritchard cajoled me into action as the cooking pot bubbled.

I have dined with kings. I have eaten snake, lizard, bat and caviar. I have drunk passion-fruit juice, yoghurt, snake's blood and claret. I have dedicated my liver to my art. No, my craft. My job? Well, anyway, I live and breathe food and drink. There is no finer recreation than sharing a table laden with food, no matter how simple or how grand, with your friends.

So the reason for this modest masterpiece is simply to share with you a selection of my favourite dishes drawn from ten years of public cooking and nearly thirty years of, as they say in the trade, standing in front of the 'piano'. And no, it's not bat and snake and it's not three-star Michelin cooking – it's just simple, fun food. That anyone who has a little patience and a lot of love can cook.

ƒOUPS

PEA AND MINT SOUP

Fresh peas and mint constitute the traditional summer flavours of British cooking. When I first wrote this recipe I was passionately committed to fresh garden peas. But unless you are able to obtain small, succulent fresh peas, you might as well use frozen *petit pois*. The mint, however, must be fresh.

SERVES 4

50g/2oz butter
675g/1½lb fresh green peas, shelled
50g/2oz plain flour
1.2 litres/2 pints chicken stock

salt and freshly ground black pepper
1 mint sprig
a little caster sugar
150ml/5fl oz double cream
chopped mint, to garnish

Melt the butter in a pan, add the peas and cook gently, covered, for 5 minutes. Blend in the flour and gradually stir in the stock; season with salt and pepper and add the mint sprig. Bring to the boil, then simmer for 10 minutes or until the peas are tender. Reserve a few of the peas for garnish.

Rub the soup through a sieve or purée in a food processor. Return the soup to the heat; correct the seasoning and add sugar to taste. Stir in the cream, but do not let the soup reach boiling point. Garnish with the reserved peas and mint and serve hot.

GAZPACHO

The beach at Torremolinos is empty. The colourful beach bars are shuttered and the white apartment blocks are still. The Mediterranean laps gently in this warm early Spanish morning as a huge yellow sun eases itself over the far horizon. The crew are setting up their equipment. I am sitting on the gunnel of a large rowing boat, waiting for the fishermen to come. A yellow pie-dog, a breed thrown back to the time of the Pharaohs, is watching too, hoping for some food. He looks sinister and his short fur is stretched tight over his protruding ribs.

Everyone is subdued this morning. Last night we all drank too much in an appalling flamenco bar in Málaga, where fat overmade-up women in their garish 'traditional' costumes stomped round one thin, black-moustached, aquiline-nosed, weasel-faced man – the sort of guy who would have played an informer in one of those black-and-white B-movies about the German occupation of France in the Second World War. He would, of course, end up being shot.

The tranquillity of the morning is shattered by the arrival of Miguel, an ebullient little chap in neatly-pressed white trousers, deck shoes, blue-and-white-hooped top, and an admiral's cap with a pair of crossed anchors perched jauntily on his head. And two older, noisy, bow-legged men with deep guttural voices, who are the fishermen.

We push the boat into the sea and with slow, powerful, rhythmic strokes we row out, in a semicircle, feeding the net out behind us as we go. One end of the net is fastened to the shore. In twenty minutes the fishermen have completed the whole arc and we are back on shore. They are fishing in a way unchanged since biblical times. Four of us in line haul in the net, haul and gather, haul and gather. Towards the end the net becomes heavier and heavier. What will it reveal? It could be overflowing with shiny sardines or anchovies or maybe even with some plump bass or fluttering, tiny fish that the Spanish call *bocorones*.

I am doing my piece to camera as we strain on the net; it is really quite a moving experience. There is still no one stirring on the Strip behind us. Finally, the net is on the beach. Excitedly, we peer down and open it to reveal thirteen tiny, pathetic little fishes.

The Plan is, or rather the Plan was, to follow up this pastiche of traditional Spanish life with a cooking sketch. And I know He did a pretty good job with just two, but there ain't much I can do with this lot. We decide to go for Plan B. Plan B centres on Miguel's idea that strong, silent men who have been going about their business in small boats at sea, spending hours toiling, should walk fifty yards to their beach bar, open it up and have a few shots of brandy while deciding what to do next.

The sun is higher now. The thick black coffee laced with *Ciento y Tres* is terrific. Holiday-makers in track suits are beginning to appear. The waiters, white shirted and black waist-coated, open up the beach bars. Beach boys are laying out the deck chairs and the sun loungers, men in little bars are peeling potatoes, preparing Spanish omelettes, chopping up peppers and filleting anchovies to pickle in olive oil. Crates are being stacked, shelves filled, baskets of olives and tomatoes are being delivered and the air is filled with the aroma of olive oil. A boy

GAZPACHO *continued*

is cleaning the beach, picking up cigarette ends and other debris.

Torremolinos, the Strip, is about to burst into another day of food, fun, sun and an awful lot of drink. And it was in the midst of this total, enjoyable, innocent, ingenuous situation that I suddenly decided to make the mother and father of all *gazpachos* in a large bucket, using a hand-held blender the size of a small outboard motor. And the secret flavour of the soup was that all the vegetables had been ripened in the hot Spanish sun. They were, as Miguel said, 'happy vegetables' and looking back on my journey through Spain with fondness, in what many dismiss as a very tacky town, this remains one of my highlights of *Floyd on Spain*.

Now for the recipe:

SERVES 12

1.5kg/3½lb fresh, ripe, really
  well-flavoured tomatoes,
  skinned and roughly chopped
2 medium green peppers,
  cored, deseeded and chopped
2 small onions, chopped
2 cucumbers, peeled and
  chopped
8 tablespoons red wine or
  sherry vinegar
1 teaspoon chopped tarragon
  or ½ teaspoon dried
½ teaspoon sugar
2 garlic cloves, chopped
225ml/8fl oz tomato juice
225ml/8fl oz iced water

salt
ice cubes

FOR THE CROÛTONS:
30g/1¼oz butter
2 slices of white bread, crusts
  removed, cut into small
  cubes
1 garlic clove, crushed
  (optional)

FOR THE SIDE DISHES:
cucumber, green pepper,
  tomatoes, onions,
  all very finely chopped

Chuck all the ingredients except the garnishes into a food processor (in several batches) and blend well. It is rather like liquidizing a salad. Check the seasoning before chilling very well.

For the croûtons, melt the butter in a heavy frying pan. Add the bread cubes and cook gently, stirring and turning well, until golden and crunchy. Drain on kitchen paper and allow to cool down. If you are a garlic fanatic, add the crushed garlic to the pan when you are frying the bread.

When you are serving the soup, pass round the garnishes and croûtons in separate little bowls.

CULLEN SKINK

Until I researched and wrote the recipes for *Floyd on Britain and Ireland* I thought that cullen skink was a species of wild Scots mountain cat, but in fact Cullen is a small village on the Moray coast and this thick fish broth or skink is a local speciality. Delicious it is too!

SERVES 4

675g/1½lb finnan haddock
  fillets, skinned
2 large onions, quartered
450g/1lb boiled potatoes, sliced
900ml/1½ pints milk
50g/2oz butter

50g/2oz plain flour
salt and freshly ground black
  pepper
50ml/2fl oz double cream
snipped chives, to garnish

Poach the haddock, onions and potatoes in the milk until cooked and all broken down. Strain and reserve the milk. Purée the fish mixture in a food processor or blender.

Melt the butter and stir in the flour. Gradually add the reserved milk, stirring; add more milk if necessary. Then add the fish mixture and season to taste with salt and pepper, taking care with the salt as the soup will already be fairly salty.

Lastly add the cream, being careful not to let the soup boil. Sprinkle with the chives and serve hot.

ALMOND CREAM SOUP

In southern Spain almonds grow as prolifically as Brussels sprouts do in Bradford. It has always been my fond hope that people would take my cookery books on holiday with them so that they can enjoy the dishes where the ingredients are native, fresh, and readily available. Do take the trouble to search for really fresh almonds. It will be well worthwhile.

SERVES 4–6

50g/2oz butter
50g/2oz plain flour
900ml/1½ pints chicken stock, preferably home-made
450ml/¾ pint milk
100g/4oz ground almonds

150ml/5fl oz single cream
1 egg yolk
salt and freshly ground white pepper
a few extra flaked and toasted almonds, to garnish

Melt the butter in a large pan and blend in the flour. Gradually whisk in the stock and milk to make a smooth, lump-free consistency. Heat until almost boiling, when the mixture will thicken to make the basis of this delicious cream soup. Turn down the heat to really low and simmer gently for 15 minutes.

Scatter in the ground almonds and stir, then cook for 5 more minutes. Now you can strain the mixture through a sieve to give a super-smooth consistency, but this is not essential.

Just before serving, whisk together the cream and egg yolk and stir through the soup. Heat gently for a moment, but do not boil otherwise it will curdle. Season to taste with salt and pepper, and sprinkle a few almonds on top. Serve hot.

SOUPE AU PISTOU

This curious, delicious, yet gutsy soup is one of the best things to have come from Provence. It is of such importance to the French kitchen and way of life that prospective mothers-in-law will query, question and interrogate their beloved son's intended as to her ability to make this soup before they will countenance giving their approval to the alliance. Stout men in bars will recount exuberantly to you the magnificence of the *Soupe au Pistou* that they had for lunch yesterday, or have in prospect for lunch today. It is a funny thing to hear French men talk in bars, *pastis* in hand, with brow furrowed in concentration – to hear them talk you would think they knew how to cook – the funny thing is, they don't! They do, however, know how to eat and as they always say in these bars, I'm telling you the absolute truth and if my wife were here she would confirm it, but of course, as you know, their wives are never there – they are at home preparing *Soupe au Pistou*.

SERVES 8

2 tablespoons olive oil
5 garlic cloves, chopped
675g/1½lb tomatoes, skinned,
  deseeded and chopped
450g/1lb fresh white haricot
  beans, shelled, or
450g/1lb dried haricot beans,
  soaked overnight (if you
  can't get fresh ones)
3 small new potatoes, scrubbed
  and chopped

450g/1lb courgettes, chopped
450g/1lb green beans, topped
  and tailed, and cut in half
450g/1lb broad beans, shelled
2 bunches of basil, chopped
2 handfuls of vermicelli
salt and freshly ground black
  pepper
Gruyère and/or Parmesan
  cheese, grated

Heat the oil in a large pan and gently fry 2 of the garlic cloves, taking care not to burn them or the garlic will become bitter. Add the tomatoes and 2 litres (3½ pints) cold salted water. Bring to the boil and add the haricots. Simmer for 15 minutes or 90 if cooking dried beans, then add the potatoes, courgettes, green beans and broad beans. Simmer for 25 minutes.

Meanwhile, pound together the basil and remaining garlic in a mortar and pestle, or in a blender, until you have a thick paste. Stir in a cupful of slightly cooled soup liquid. Add to the rest of the soup. Throw in the vermicelli. Season to taste with salt and pepper and cook for about 5–10 minutes, or until the pasta is tender. Serve with grated Gruyère or Parmesan cheese. You can make more of the basil and garlic mixture if you wish and serve it separately so the diners can add more if they like it – which they should.

PS In my view, you can't have too much basil in this soup and you can add another dash of olive oil at the last minute.

CRAB CHOWDER

I have to admit that most chowders, from a purist's point of view, tend to be a bit of a culinary cop-out, but there are times when, say, a crab chowder, a mussel chowder or a lobster chowder taste really good and they are easy to prepare and very quick – really useful for people with busy lives and tight schedules. This recipe comes from one of those wonderful Louisiana motel/gas station/diners, all chrome and Formica with Cajun music on the juke box. I loved it – but if you want a serious fish soup, see the recipe for Italian Fish Soup (page 16).

SERVES 4–6

5 tablespoons butter
5 tablespoons plain flour
600ml/1 pint milk
450ml/¾ pint chicken stock
25g/1oz onion, finely chopped
175g/6oz fresh or frozen
    crabmeat

1 x 350g/12oz can of sweet-
    corn, drained
salt and freshly ground black
    pepper
a large pinch of cayenne pepper
100ml/4fl oz double cream

In a saucepan melt 4 tablespoons of the butter and beat in the flour. Add the milk and stock, whisking all the time. Cook for about 10 minutes, stirring constantly. In a separate saucepan melt the remaining butter, add the onion and cook until soft. Put in the crabmeat, corn and seasoning. Heat through and add to the chowder. Stir in the cream. Bring to simmering point and simmer very gently for about 5 minutes.

HOT AND SOUR SEAFOOD SOUP

This tangy and refreshing soup is light and nutritious; it will revive you after a heavy night out; it will nourish you without damaging your waistline. If you want to bulk it out, add some noodles at the end – they only take a minute or two to cook.

SERVES 4

1 litre/1¾ pints chicken stock
1 blade of lemon grass, finely sliced
2.5cm/1in piece of galangal or fresh root ginger, thinly sliced
2–3 Kaffir lime leaves
450g/1lb king prawns, peeled and deveined, leaving tail ends intact
1 x 425g/15oz can of straw mushrooms, drained and quartered

fresh coconut slivers (from about ¼ coconut)
1 tablespoon lime juice
2 teaspoons fish sauce
2 teaspoons chilli paste
bird's-eye chilli peppers, deseeded and thinly sliced, to garnish
coriander leaves, to garnish

Heat the stock in a pan over a medium heat. Add the lemon grass, galangal and lime leaves. Bring to the boil, then throw in the prawns, mushrooms and coconut. Simmer gently until the prawns turn pink and are tender.

Meanwhile, mix together the lime juice, fish sauce and chilli paste. Stir this mixture into the soup when the prawns are cooked. Heat through for a minute or two, then serve sprinkled with the chilli peppers and coriander leaves.

ITALIAN FISH SOUP

A fine lunch dish for those warm summer days is a piping hot fresh fish soup. This Italian version is simple and quick. You will need one or two kilos of strong-flavoured, firm-fleshed fish, for example, eel, monkfish, octopus, red snapper, large prawns or dogfish. You can use any fish you like, there are no rules and the best way to do this is to wander around a busy fish market and become inspired. When I first cooked this soup it was in the middle of a street next to the Grand Canal in Venice and had I listened to the advice of the assembled bunch of morning shoppers, telephone engineers and gondoliers, we would have had twenty differing versions of this recipe. Everyone had a view! 'More garlic – more olive oil – don't use monkfish' etc., etc. Anyway, this is an authentic *burrida*.

SERVES 6–8

90ml/3fl oz olive oil
1 small onion, finely chopped
1 small carrot, finely diced
2 celery sticks, finely chopped
1kg/2¼lb ripe plum tomatoes, skinned, deseeded and chopped
3–4 anchovy fillets, chopped
1 tablespoon chopped basil
1 tablespoon chopped parsley, flat-leaf if possible
2–3 garlic cloves, finely chopped

salt and freshly ground black pepper
1.5 litres/2½ pints hot water
2kg/4½lb firm-fleshed fish, filleted and cut into large pieces (choose from a mixture of eels, monkfish, squid, octopus, scampi tails, red snapper, etc.) – ask your fishmonger to prepare it
chopped basil and parsley, to garnish

Heat the oil in a very large saucepan or flameproof casserole and sauté the onion for about 3–4 minutes until lightly browned. Add the carrot and celery and sauté for a few more minutes, then add the tomatoes and the anchovies (optional). Stir well, then add the basil, parsley and garlic. Season with salt and pepper. Pour in the hot water and bring to the boil.

If you are using octopus or squid, add to the pan, cover and cook for about 25 minutes before adding the rest of the fish, then cook for about 20 more minutes.

Ladle the stew into warmed bowls and garnish with the basil and parsley.

STILTON AND CAULIFLOWER SOUP

This soup, once a clichéd mainstay on any wine bar menu, does in fact stand up as a classic.

Serves 4

15g/½oz butter
1 onion, chopped
1 cauliflower, broken into florets
600ml/1 pint light chicken or
   vegetable stock
1 bouquet garni
salt and freshly ground white
   pepper

1 tablespoon cornflour
300ml/½ pint milk
100g/4oz blue Stilton cheese,
   crumbled
chopped parsley, to garnish

Melt the butter in a pan, add the onion and fry until soft. Add the cauliflower, stock, bouquet garni, and salt and pepper to taste. Bring up to the boil, then cover and simmer for 15 minutes; cool slightly. Remove the bouquet garni.

Sieve the soup or purée in a food processor or blender. Blend the cornflour with 2 tablespoons of the milk. Add to the purée with the remaining milk. Bring to the boil again, stirring. Remove from the heat and stir in the cheese until well mixed in. Garnish with the parsley and serve hot.

CURRIED PARSNIP SOUP

SERVES 4

50g/2oz butter
1 onion, finely chopped
900g/2lb parsnips, chopped
1 heaped tablespoon mild curry
   powder
600ml/1 pint chicken stock

salt and freshly ground black
   pepper
juice of ½ lemon
2 egg yolks
150ml/5fl oz double cream

Melt the butter in a large pan and sweat the onion for 2 minutes. Add the parsnips and cook for about 5 minutes or until softened. Stir in the curry powder and stock. Bring to the boil, then simmer for 15–20 minutes or until the parsnips are tender.

Purée the soup in a food processor or blender and return it to a clean pan. Season to taste with salt and pepper, add the lemon juice and reheat the soup until hot but not boiling. Whisk together the egg yolks and cream and gradually stir into the soup. On no account allow to boil. Serve hot.

FISH AND SHELLFISH

HAKE WITH POTATOES AND GARLIC

It was a hot day and after a long journey across the Spanish countryside in a pathetic little car without air conditioning, I was tired, thirsty and irritable, and not at all in the mood for monasteries. Then, as I rounded a bend on this tortuous road, the land dropped away to reveal a serene valley and an impressive granite monastery dating from the fifteenth century, set in neatly cultivated vegetable gardens.

But as we approached the front of the edifice I was astounded to see a massive coach park, souvenir shops, bars and throngs of people milling about smoking, drinking and eating, for all the world as if they were visiting Disneyland. You could buy holy honey, holy wine, holy candles, holy cassettes of the monks' greatest hits, Gregorian chants volumes 1 and 2, and all manner of holy artifacts.

I hadn't realized that monasteries are big business these days. And I felt, I must say, a little upset, a little cheated by this brash commercial approach to support what I had always assumed was the quiet, self-sacrificial, contemplative life. So, with thoughts of the old jingle 'I am but a poor wandering monk with only one dirty habit' racing through my mind, I swung jauntily on the massive bell-pull and waited to be admitted.

A long way off a bell rang and reverberated in some far-off cloister, and minutes passed before heavy bolts slipped back and the huge door opened to reveal a mild, gentle-looking monk who shook my hand and bade me come in.

My judgement had been hasty and incorrect. Within the monastery proper, quiet, genial and sincere men went about their work and their devotions with integrity and commitment. In fact, this place, the Cistercian Monastery of Osera, is I think where Graham Greene often retreated.

Normally, when we are away filming, we are a noisy, irreverent bunch, fond of telling rude jokes and using pretty bad language. But here we behaved perfectly, I am pleased to say, and felt spiritually cleansed by this brief encounter with people who had given up – or had never contemplated – jet-setting around the world slurping champagne and eating caviar, as is my unhappy lot.

Anyway, I cooked them some poached hake and promised to return one day, without cameras and the temporary glitz of a film crew.

SERVES 4

1 onion, peeled and halved (for flavour only)

1 red pepper, cored, deseeded and sliced lengthways

1 green or yellow pepper, cored, deseeded and sliced lengthways

8 potatoes, sliced

4 x 175g/6oz hake cutlets

6 tablespoons olive oil

4 garlic cloves, crushed

2 heaped tablespoons paprika

lemon wedges, to garnish

HAKE WITH POTATOES AND GARLIC *continued*

Bring two pans of salted water to the boil and add half an onion to each. Put the peppers into one pan and the potatoes into the other. Bring to the boil and simmer for 10 minutes. Now add the fish cutlets to the peppers and poach gently for 5 minutes – remember, always slightly undercook fish. Drain the fish, peppers and potatoes and keep warm.

To make the sauce, heat the oil in a frying pan and gently fry the garlic for a couple of minutes, making sure it doesn't burn. This forms the basis of the sauce. Take the pan off the heat, wait for a moment, then stir in the paprika, blending it in well. Let it settle, so that the paprika will flavour the oil.

Layer the cooked potatoes, peppers and poached hake on a warmed serving dish and spoon the flavoured aromatic oil over the top. Garnish with the lemon wedges and serve immediately.

HERRINGS WITH BACON

As a child I loved to eat a hot herring baked in vinegar, cloves and onions for supper on Saturday night, or a crisply fried herring for breakfast with doorsteps of warm, crusty bread and butter. But now they are rare and quite a treat.

SERVES 4

8 x 150g/5oz fresh herrings
juice of 2 lemons
salt
2 tablespoons mild mustard

16 rashers of rindless streaky
   bacon
100ml/4fl oz oil

Dehead, slit, clean, scale, wash and dry the herrings. Then, with forefinger and thumb inside the fish under the centre spine, take out as many bones as you can without ripping the flesh.

Fold the herrings out flat. Brush the insides with lemon juice and sprinkle with salt. Next, spread a little mustard on each fish, close and wrap each in 2 rashers of bacon, using a wooden cocktail stick to hold the bacon in place.

Now cook the herrings in the oil in a shallow frying pan for about 6 minutes on each side until the bacon is golden and the herrings cooked. Do not have the oil too hot to begin with, or the bacon will be cremated before the herrings are cooked.

Pat off excess fat with kitchen paper and serve with a really fresh, crisp, mixed salad of raw fennel, tomatoes, red and white cabbage or any gutsy, crunchy combination of vegetables you fancy. And why not use this dish as an excuse to drink near-frozen vodka or aquavit with lager chasers?

RED MULLET WITH PESTO

One of the finest of fish is the red mullet, but scale and gut them carefully, leaving the liver intact – it's delicious. As with so many dishes, the exact ingredients of pesto vary from region to region and family to family. You might like to add a little more lemon juice or more or less garlic, it depends on your taste.

SERVES 4

FOR THE PESTO SAUCE:
2–3 garlic cloves
50g/2oz pine nuts
1 large bunch of basil
1 large bunch of parsley,
   flat-leaf if possible
about 6 tablespoons olive oil

350g/12oz fresh pasta, such as
   tagliatelle, fettucine, linguine
5 tablespoons olive oil
a good pinch of salt
4 red mullet, cleaned and scaled
a good squeeze of lemon juice
2 lemons, halved, to serve

First make the pesto sauce by pounding together the garlic and pine nuts in a mortar and pestle. Tear the basil and parsley leaves from their stalks and add them to the mixture, pounding them down well. Slowly drizzle in the oil and mix until well blended. All this can be done in a food processor or blender if you want to save time. The pesto should look like a thickish mint sauce.

Put a big pan of water on to cook the pasta, adding 2 tablespoons of the oil and a good pinch of salt to flavour it. When the water is boiling, add the pasta and cook until just tender – al dente.

Meanwhile, fry the mullet in 3 tablespoons of the remaining oil for about 7 minutes, turning it over once and adding the lemon juice. Spoon the pesto sauce on top of the fish and serve with the lemon halves and cooked, drained pasta.

SALT COD WITH CHICK PEAS

A kilometre outside Toledo, on top of a hill, there is a parador with an enormous terrace, from which there is a spectacular view of the city with its towers, battlements, churches and castles. The parador staff were kind enough to let me use their kitchen and there I prepared a dish using one of my favourite – and certainly one of the Spanish people's favourite – salt cod.

Ah, salt cod! I have fond memories of the Fridays of my childhood when the fishmonger set up his stall and we would buy great sheets of salted, dried cod. Teafish as it was known. It was soaked in water all Saturday and poached in milk for breakfast on Sunday with a big knob of salty farmhouse butter and lots of pepper.

Before refrigeration, salting was one of the main methods of preserving food and the tradition lives happily on because the thick, salted slabs of firm-fleshed milky-white cod make it unquestionably one of the greatest fish available. The salting makes it slightly tougher than fresh cod, but gives it a more meaty texture. After it has been soaked overnight in water and well rinsed to remove the salt, it has a unique flavour.

Incidentally, many bars in Spain offer as an excellent *tapa* a little cube of raw salt cod stuck with a toothpick to a fresh raw broad bean.

The dish that I quote below would long ago probably just have been cod and potatoes stewed together. But the Arab contribution of chick peas and spinach makes it really interesting.

SERVES 4–6

450g/1lb chick peas, soaked
   for 24 hours
450g/1lb salt cod, soaked for
   24 hours and cut into pieces
225g/8oz potatoes, cut into
   small chunks
6 tablespoons olive oil
2 garlic cloves, chopped

1 thick slice of bread, crusts
   removed
a few saffron strands
225g/8oz fresh spinach, well
   washed and trimmed
salt and freshly ground black
   pepper

Drain the chick peas and salt cod, rinsing both in fresh water. Now put the chick peas into a large flameproof cooking pot with some cold water and bring to the boil, then simmer gently for about 1½ hours until almost cooked, adding the salt cod and spuds after about 1 hour.

When they are nearly done, heat the oil in a frying pan and sauté the garlic and bread until both are golden-brown. Drain on kitchen paper, then pound them down with the saffron to make a glorious golden paste.

Cook the spinach briefly in a tiny amount of water, drain well and squeeze out the excess liquid. Chop it up a bit and fry in what is left of the oil, then add it to the chick peas and salt cod.

Go back to your golden paste and add a little hot water. Mix it through, then add to the pot with the chick peas and fish. Simmer everything together for 10 minutes or so, until the sauce thickens and is golden. Taste it and season. I am sure you will need some pepper but go easy on the salt.

FLOYD'S TASMANIA ON A PLATE

If you find yourself in Australia it is worthwhile taking a trip to Tasmania. Although it looks like a little island on the map, it is about the same size as Ireland. It is pretty, unspoiled and fun. Unusually for me, I had a successful day's fishing and caught eight large tuna. The owner of the boat gave me one and I took it to Mures Restaurant in Hobart and prepared this dish.

SERVES 4

4 or 6 x 150g/6oz tuna
   steaks
olive oil

FOR THE ANCHOVY BUTTER:
100g/4oz butter, softened
6 anchovy fillets in oil, drained
   and chopped
squeeze of lemon juice
1 teaspoon dill, finely chopped
freshly ground black pepper

FOR THE TOMATO CONCASSE:
4 ripe tomatoes, skinned and
   finely chopped
1 small onion, finely chopped
½ red pepper, deseeded and
   finely chopped
1 garlic clove, crushed
1 tablespoon olive oil
freshly ground black pepper

Rinse the tuna steaks really well to remove any traces of blood. Drain on absorbent paper.

Beat together all the ingredients for the anchovy butter until smooth and well blended, or whizz in a blender. Form into a roll on a piece of greaseproof paper or foil and chill for about 15 minutes until firm.

Make the tomato concasse by cooking together the tomatoes, onion, red pepper, garlic and olive oil in a pan over a gentle heat for 20 minutes. Season to taste with black pepper and keep warm.

To cook the fish, brush a large, heavy-based frying pan with olive oil, heat for a moment until really hot, then seal the tuna steaks on each side over a high heat. Cook for about 2 minutes on each side, reducing the heat. Be careful not to overcook the fish – they should be cooked as medium-rare steaks, but sauté for longer if you really do prefer them cooked through.

Put a good spoonful of the hot tomato concasse on to warmed serving plates. Lay the tuna on top and then put a good dollop of anchovy butter on to each fillet. Serve immediately with steaming saffron rice.

WHOLE FRIED FISH WITH GINGER AND SPRING ONIONS

A perfect way of cooking any fish but particularly good for bream, mullet, red snapper or even freshwater perch. The dish is of Chinese origin but you will find similar ones throughout south-east Asia.

Score the whole fish first to prevent it from bursting and to enable the flesh to absorb easily the flavours of the seasoning and sauce.

SERVES 4

675g/1½lb fish, cleaned and
  scaled
1 teaspoon salt
2 tablespoons plain flour
3 tablespoons vegetable oil
3–4 spring onions, trimmed and
  cut into 2.5cm/1in lengths
2.5cm/1in piece of fresh root
  ginger, shredded
coriander leaves or parsley, to
  garnish

FOR THE SAUCE:
2 tablespoons soy sauce
2 tablespoons dry sherry or
  white wine
150ml/5fl oz chicken stock or
  cold water
1 teaspoon cornflour
freshly ground black pepper

Using a sharp knife, slash the fish diagonally 2–3 times on each side, sprinkle with salt and roll in the flour to coat. Heat the oil in a large frying pan or wok until almost smoking, then add the fish. Reduce the heat a little and fry the fish for about 2–3 minutes on each side, until it is crisp and golden on the outside and the flesh is deliciously moist but firm. Carefully lift out the fish from the pan.

Quickly mix together all the sauce ingredients. Add the spring onions and ginger to the oil remaining in the pan and stir-fry for about 30 seconds. Stir in the sauce and return the fish to the pan. Bubble away for a couple of minutes, then lift the fish on to a warmed serving plate. Pour over the sauce and garnish with coriander or parsley. Serve with plain boiled rice or noodles.

THAI FISH CAKES AND CUCUMBER SALAD

A perfect light lunch or supper, with an authentic taste of Thailand, that is easy to prepare.

MAKES ABOUT 10–12

450g/1lb fillets of firm white fish, such as cod or haddock, skinned
1–2 tablespoons red curry paste
1 egg, beaten
2 teaspoons fish sauce
a handful of Kaffir lime leaves and basil leaves, finely chopped
a little plain flour for dredging
groundnut or sunflower oil for deep-frying

Put the fish, curry paste and egg into a food processor and whizz until smooth. Add the fish sauce and whizz again – don't let the mixture become too runny. Add the lime and basil leaves.

With your hands form the mixture into small cakes about 5cm/2in wide. Dredge well with flour. Deep-fry in a wok in 2.5cm/1in hot oil for a few minutes until crisp and golden.

CUCUMBER SALAD

1 cucumber, peeled, deseeded
  and grated
2–3 red chilli peppers, deseeded
  and chopped
2–3 shallots, grated

2 tablespoons fish sauce
2 tablespoons dried prawn
  powder
juice of ½ lemon or lime

Put all the ingredients into a bowl, mix well together and serve.

TUNA STEAKS WITH ANCHOVY AND FENNEL BUTTER

For a fish like tuna it's nice to have a little salsa with it as well. Finely chop some ripe tomatoes (but not so fine that they turn to a mush) and dice some crisp spring onions and shallots. Mix lightly with a little chopped flat-leaf parsley and add lemon juice to taste.

SERVES 4

4 × 175–200g/6–7oz tuna steaks
175g/6oz butter, softened
3 anchovy fillets in oil, drained
  and chopped

2 teaspoons fennel seeds or a
  small handful of fresh fennel
  fronds
freshly ground black pepper
2 tablespoons vegetable oil

Wash the tuna steaks well, and pat dry with absorbent paper. Make the flavoured butter by beating together the butter, anchovies and fennel seeds or fronds with a little pepper, or whizz in a food processor or blender. Form the butter into a roll on a piece of greaseproof paper and refrigerate for about 15 minutes until firm.

Heat the oil in a large frying pan and brown the tuna steaks on both sides for about 2 minutes. Reduce the heat and cook the fish gently for 8 minutes or so, turning once, until it flakes easily.

Pop a roundel of anchovy butter on top of each tuna steak and serve with the tomato salsa.

BASS FLAMED WITH FENNEL AND ARMAGNAC

In high summer in Provence you take bundles of wild fennel stalks and leave them to dry in the sun so that later you can burn a faggot of fennel under that supreme fish – the bass – giving it the heady aromatic flavour of the Midi. A classic among classics. This must be cooked on a barbecue.

Serves 6

1 bass at least 1.35kg/3lb, scaled, gutted and cleaned
1 teaspoon sea salt
freshly ground black pepper
olive oil

1 bundle of dried fennel stalks, as big in volume though not in weight as the fish
2 liqueur glasses of Armagnac or eau de vie
3 lemons, halved, to serve

Wash the bass and dry carefully. Slash diagonal cuts into both sides and rub the salt into the cuts and skin. Liberally grind pepper over and inside the fish and then brush with oil.

Grill the bass over a barbecue, turning from time to time, for about 20 minutes, depending on the size of the fish.

Meanwhile, erect a griddle or wire stand on an oval fireproof tray and stack the fennel stalks underneath it. When the fish is cooked, transfer it to the stand, pour the alcohol over the fish and fennel stalks and ignite. Leave to burn until the stalks have burnt away – this will impart the most superb flavour and is spectacularly dazzling as you transport the bass in flames to the table, garn-ished with the lemon halves.

ROAST MONKFISH WITH GARLIC

As fish go, the monk is not high up in the glamour stakes; in fact, it is downright ugly. But God clearly knew what he was doing when he created the flesh – it is absolutely fine. It has the flavour of shellfish – exquisite. If you have a big piece, or tail as it is known, you can roast it as if it were a leg of lamb.

SERVES 4

1kg/2¼lb monkfish tail
2 bulbs of plump garlic
thin slices of streaky bacon
3 tablespoons olive oil
salt and freshly ground black
  pepper

¼ teaspoon thyme leaves
¼ teaspoon fennel seeds
juice of 1 lemon
1 bay leaf
grilled tomatoes, to serve

Skin the monkfish carefully, leaving no trace of the thin membrane under the skin, and remove the central bone.

Peel 2 cloves of garlic and cut into thin slices. Make some incisions in the monkfish and push in the garlic slices. Wrap the fish in the bacon and secure with cocktail sticks.

Heat 2 tablespoons of the oil in a frying pan and brown the fish on all sides for 5 minutes. Season with salt, pepper, thyme, fennel and lemon juice and put into a baking tray along with the remaining oil. Arrange the remaining unpeeled garlic around the dish, pop the bay leaf under the fish and cook in the oven preheated to 220°C/425°F/gas mark 7 for 20 minutes. Serve with grilled tomatoes. Encourage your guests to overcome any reticence to eat the roasted garlic.

BREAM WITH FRESH HERBS

There is the red bream and the black bream. The red is more delicious. Check for bright, shiny eyes and a fresh pinkness behind the gills. Be sure to trim the fins and scale them.

SERVES 4

1 bream, at least x 900g/2lb,
  scaled, gutted and cleaned
3 tablespoons oil
salt and freshly ground black
  pepper
1 thyme sprig

1 bay leaf
3 spring onions, chopped
200ml/7fl oz dry white wine
2 fresh fennel fronds, chopped
1 tablespoon chopped parsley

Wash the bream and dry it carefully.

Grease an overproof dish with some of the oil. Season the bream inside and out with salt and pepper and put the thyme and bay leaf inside the fish. Pop the bream into the dish, add the spring onions and the remaining oil and cook in the oven preheated to 220°C/425°F /gas mark 7 for 15 minutes.

Add the wine, fennel and parsley and cook for 15 more minutes or until cooked through. Remove the bay leaf before serving.

FILLET OF SALMON WITH WATERCRESS SAUCE

Well, it had to happen. Salmon is now more plentiful and cheaper than the noble cod. This is as a result of highly successful salmon farming. Good luck and well done I say, but as good as they are, these farmed ones, nothing can compare with the firm-flaked flesh from a freshly landed salmon pulled from an Irish lough that you yourself have hooked on a fine Hardy rod with a Golden Prince reel. Actually, I am fantasizing here; the last fresh Irish salmon I hooked was landed by the gillie on a fifty-year-old, tatty rod with loose ferrules and backing line. So much for being a poseur. However, he did admire my deerstalker! Anyway, back to cooking. The point I am trying to make is do try to get wild salmon if at all possible. Check with your supplier how long he has had the fish because salmon does benefit from having been 'hung' for a couple of days.

PS Since writing I actually did land my first Irish salmon with my friend Mike Powel at Castleconnel on the Shannon in Co. Limerick – great place for fishing.

SERVES 4

4 bunches of watercress
25g/1oz butter
50g/2oz shallots, chopped
4 x 200g/7oz fresh salmon
   fillets

salt and freshly ground black
   pepper
225ml/8fl oz dry white wine
225ml/8fl oz fish stock
100ml/4fl oz double cream

Wash and pick over the watercress. Discard the stalks. Put the watercress into a pan of boiling water and blanch for 1 minute. Drain, refresh under cold running water and drain again. Purée in a food processor or blender until smooth. Set aside.

Lightly butter a roasting tin and cover the base with the shallots. Place the salmon on top and season to taste with salt and pepper. Pour in the wine and stock. Cover with foil or a butter wrapper and cook in the oven preheated to 160°C/325°F/gas mark 3 for about 8–10 minutes, depending on the thickness of the fish – do not overcook. Lift out the salmon, cover with the foil or wrapper and keep warm.

Pour the juices and stock into a clean pan and boil briskly until reduced to 150ml/5fl oz. Add the cream, bring to a simmer, and cook until the sauce is of a thin coating consistency. Just before serving, add the watercress purée (if you add it too early it will discolour and lose its lovely green appearance). Check and adjust the seasoning if necessary.

To serve, arrange the salmon on warmed plates and pour over the sauce.

MONGOLIAN FISH HOTPOT

This is not only a gastronomic treat of the utmost delicacy but also a visual delight, and although you can use your cast-iron fondue set to boil the stock in at the table, it would be much better to buy the correct Mongolian Fire or Chafing Pot. It comes with little wire baskets with which you can fish out your merry morsels. You also need small bowls for the sauces, bowls to eat from and chopsticks to eat with. And because at the end of the banquet you should drink the liquid in which the fish has been cooked, you will also need china spoons.

All the specialist ingredients for the Mongolian Fish Hotpot can be obtained from a Chinese supermarket.

SERVES 6–8

1.35kg/3lb freshest raw fish,
perhaps a mixture of: fresh
scallops, halved crossways,
thin slivers of squid, whole
large prawns, peeled, with
heads and tails left on, thin
fillets of lemon or Dover
sole, skinned, fork-sized
cubes of salmon

450g/1lb young spinach leaves

225g/8oz broccoli spears, with
thin-trimmed stalks

900g/2lb Chinese cabbage, cut
into pieces

100g/4oz transparent noodles,
soaked in water for 10 minutes
and drained

12 slices of beancurd cake

FOR THE DIPS:

hoisin sauce

chilli sauce

2 parts soy sauce mixed with
1 part sesame oil

4 parts finely chopped spring
onion mixed with 1 part
finely chopped fresh ginger
and garlic

TO SERVE:

2.4 litres/4 pints water

dash of fish sauce

2 chicken stock cubes

To serve, bring the water and fish sauce to the boil and dissolve
the stock cubes in it. Using their little wire baskets as nets,
guests can dip fish, vegetables, noodles and beancurd cake alter-
nately into the bubbling liquid for 20–30 seconds and then dip
into one of the four dips as they choose.

When all the fish has gone, add the remaining vegetables to
the boiling pot, and if necessary more water, and serve as soup.

CHILLI-HOT SQUID WITH VEGETABLES

While filming in Italy I spent a night on an eighteen-foot fishing boat, creeping around the Ligurian coast, peering through a sort of bucket with a glass bottom, looking for squid. As we located them, the fishermen speared them with a trident and in the morning they were taken to the fish market and no doubt dipped in batter and deep-fried. Nice as it is that way, here is a spicy alternative.

Serves 4

450g/1lb squid – ask your fishmonger to clean and prepare it for you or do this yourself (see opposite)

2 tablespoons vegetable oil

1 small green pepper cored, deseeded and thinly sliced into rings

1 small red pepper, cored, deseeded and thinly sliced into rings

1 onion, finely chopped

2 garlic cloves, crushed

1 or 2 red or green chilli peppers, deseeded and finely chopped

2 teaspoons caster sugar

salt and freshly ground black pepper

Chinese leaves, spinach, broccoli, green beans, to stir-fry

Cut the squid into 2.5cm/1in pieces, scoring the flesh in a diamond pattern to tenderize it. Heat the oil in a large frying pan or wok and fry the peppers and onion together for 2 minutes. Pop in the squid, garlic, chillies and sugar and stir-fry for 2–3 more minutes, stirring constantly. Season with salt and pepper and serve immediately, with plain boiled rice and some quickly stir-fried Chinese leaves, spinach, broccoli, green beans or any crunchy green vegetable.

PREPARING SQUID

Squid, often called calamari or ink-fish, are usually sold whole by weight, though you can sometimes buy squid 'rings' – the sliced body pouch. If your fishmonger isn't too busy, you may be able to charm him or her into doing the messy bits for you.

Right, line up your squid. Cut off their tentacles and set aside – yes, you do eat these. Gently pull their heads off and discard, along with the eyes, innards and ink sac. Take out the quill from inside the body pouch – it looks like a piece of transparent plastic – and wash away all the white fluid. You should now be left with the body pouch or 'hood', which has two triangular fins, and the tentacles. At the base of the tentacles is the 'beak' or mouth – take it out and chuck out.

The hood or pouch can be stuffed or sliced into rings, or it can be cut into squares and scored with a diamond pattern to tenderize it. The tentacles are usually sliced and cooked. Sometimes the ink is reserved from the ink sac and used in recipes.

MOULES À LA MARINIÈRE

A waiter with a black waistcoat and a long white apron is unfolding chairs around the tables on the pavement in front of the restaurant. It is 11.30 and the morning sun is quickly drying the freshly rinsed paving stones. A plump, prim, neat, middle-aged lady, thick, black hair swept back into a bun, is briskly laying heavy-plated cutlery on the crisp white tablecloths. A young girl with a tray is placing stainless steel cruet sets behind her. Inside, at the cool bar, I am sitting sipping a glass of *Cinquante et Un*, munching big black olives. Through the kitchen door, which is ajar, I watch chefs weighing baskets brimming with bass, mullet and bream and others piled high with shiny, black mussels. There is a *vivier* full of crayfish. It is Provence. It is summer. The town clock strikes its tinny bell twelve times. It is lunchtime and I am about to tuck into a huge white porcelain terrine filled with mussels cooked in white wine.

SERVES 6

2.5kg/5lb mussels, cleaned and bearded
freshly ground black pepper
8 garlic cloves, 2 shallots and 1 small bunch of parsley, finely chopped together

1.2 litres/2 pints Muscadet
1 bouquet garni (thyme, bay leaf and tarragon)
50g/2oz butter, cut into small chunks

Put the mussels into a large saucepan. Season generously with pepper. Add the chopped garlic, shallots and parsley. Pour in the wine, add the bouquet garni, cover and cook over a high heat for 8 minutes. Shake the pan well to make sure that all the mussels are opened. Discard any that are not. Add the butter and cook for 5 more minutes. Remove the bouquet garni. Serve the mussels immediately, with their juice.

MUSSELS AND CLAMS IN TOMATO AND WINE SAUCE

One bright blustery morning we toddled out of the harbour at O Grove in Galicia on an open fishing boat, *Silvana Os*, to harvest mussels from rickety wooden contraptions a bit like miniature oil rigs, from which are suspended loads of ropes that the mussels attach themselves to. And for those of you who like statistics, a local lad told me 90 per cent of Spain's mussels come from around this part of the Sunshine Coast and they take three years to mature to commercial standards. There are 520 platforms with hundreds of ropes on each and 120 kilos of mussels on each full rope.

To add some interest to the sketch, though, we decided to cook for Paco, the captain, and for his black dog, who ended up eating much of the offering, because Captain Paco was a bit of a Spanish chauvinist and said though my dish was okay it was not really spicy enough. Truth of the matter was he was overawed and tongue-tied by being famous for fifteen minutes on a television programme. Well, that's my story and I'm sticking to it.

SERVES 6–8

1.8g/4lb mussels, cleaned and
  bearded
450g/1lb baby clams
  (if available), cleaned
150ml/5fl oz olive oil
900g/2lb onions, sliced
6 garlic cloves, chopped into
  hefty chunks
2 bay leaves
2 tablespoons paprika

2–3 generous wine-glasses of
  dry white wine (I used Casal
  Caeiro)
900ml/1½ pints Fresh Tomato
  Sauce (see page 159)
salt and freshly ground black
  pepper
lots of chopped parsley, to
  garnish

First, find a lidded pan big enough to take all the ingredients. Throw out any mussels and clams (if using) that are broken or that do not close when handled.

Heat the oil in the pan, add the onions and garlic and fry for a couple of minutes, giving them a good stir. Cover and let the onions sweat it out for about 20 minutes.

Now chuck in all the remaining ingredients and stir. Cover and bring to the boil, shaking the pan a couple of times to redistribute the mussels and clams. Cook for 2–3 minutes more, by which time all the shells should have opened. If any don't, throw them away.

Serve at once in warmed bowls, with plenty of chopped parsley sprinkled over the top. Give your guests lots of fresh, crusty bread to mop up all the wonderful juices.

SIZZLING SCALLOPS

This recipe comes from my 'Cheat's Repertoire'. It is quick to prepare, draws upon bottled spices and sauces that we tend to keep in our cupboards, requires no skill and actually tastes dead good.

Serves 6

450g/1lb scallops, removed
   from shells and washed
1 tablespoon light soy sauce
1 tablespoon dry sherry
2 tablespoons vegetable oil
1 large onion, sliced
1 teaspoon chopped fresh root
   ginger

For the sauce:
2 teaspoons red curry past
2 teaspoons hoisin sauce
1 teaspoon sesame oil
½ teaspoon five spice powder
1 teaspoon sugar
3 teaspoons peanut butter
3 tablespoons fish stock, or
   mixed dry white wine
   and water

Trim away the crescent-shaped muscle from each scallop, then put the scallops into a non-aluminium bowl and add the soy sauce and sherry. Leave to marinate for 30 minutes or so, stirring from time to time. Meanwhile, mix together the sauce ingredients.

Heat the oil in a large frying pan or wok and stir-fry the onion for about 1 minute. Tip in the ginger, scallops and marinade and stir-fry for 2–3 minutes. Stir in the sauce mixture and heat until boiling. Serve immediately with plain boiled rice.

OYSTER PO-BOY

On my first visit to New Orleans I was intrigued to discover a
local speciality called Oyster Po-Boy. Now, my idea of heaven
is a dozen or eighteen freshly opened, native oysters, liberally
sprinkled with lemon juice, a dash of Tabasco and a grind or
two of black pepper, some good brown bread and butter and a
pint of stout. So when I discovered that Oyster Po-Boy is, in
fact, an oyster sandwich, I was a little taken aback – until I tried
one. They're terrific.

SERVES 6

2 thick French loaves
a little butter
4 dozen oysters, removed from
    shells
cornmeal for dusting

salt and freshly ground black
    pepper
oil for deep-frying
Tabasco sauce
dill pickle (pickled gherkins),
    sliced

Cut the loaves in half lengthways. Toast each half and spread
with a little butter. Dust the oysters with cornmeal, salt and
pepper, and deep-fry in hot oil for a few minutes. Make a sandwich with the toast and oysters, sprinkled with Tabasco sauce
and dill pickle.

POTTED CRAB

It is a risky business to buy a precooked crab (and frozen crab-meat is out of the question for Potted Crab), so buy a live one and cook it yourself. If possible, it should be cooked in seawater with a couple of tablespoons of extra salt added. So, simply pop your live crab into cold salted water and bring to the boil. Immediately reduce the heat and gently simmer for 10 minutes. Then switch off the heat and leave the crab in the water until cool.

To open the crab, first twist off the claws and legs. Then separate the body from the shell. Remember that as well as the brown and white meat in the body, you will discover a considerable amount of delicious flesh in the compart-mentalized chine. The inedible parts of a crab are the lungs and the sac, which should be discarded. Crack the claws to remove the meat. Use the cleaned shell as a dish for the crabmeat.

Simple fresh crab served this way, with salad, lemon juice and a good mayonnaise is superb. I don't think that hot crab dishes with cheese sauces, etc., are really worth the trouble. If you ever come across spider crabs, snap them up. Cook them the same way, but only eat the claws, which are full of succulent meat, and use an aïoli (see page 161) instead of mayonnaise.

Serves 4–5

1 large crab
a pinch of freshly grated nutmeg
salt and freshly ground black
pepper

juice of 1 lemon
1 teaspoon chilli sauce
100g/4oz butter

Take all the meat from the crab (which you have cooked yourself: see page 50) and season well with nutmeg, salt and pepper, lemon juice and chilli sauce. Mix well together and pack into ramekins. Melt half the butter and pour evenly over the ramekins. Place in a bain-marie, and bake in the oven preheated to 150°C/300°F/gas mark 3 for 20 minutes.

Leave until almost cool, then top up the ramekins with the remaining butter, clarified, and allow to set.

Serve with a crisp green salad dressed with a sharp vinaigrette.

PRAWNS DOWN UNDER

One day I was nonchalantly leaning over the stern rail of an elegant yacht, peering at the Great Barrier Reef in eastern Australia. I decided to put on a snorkel and flippers and jump in to explore the reef more closely. I am not a strong swimmer and had never snorkelled before and I very nearly drowned – which many of you may have been very pleased to hear! Choking, trembling and terrified, I was eventually hoisted back on to the yacht and after a steadying draught of Dr Johnny Walker's patented Black Label medicine, I was quickly restored to rude health. Thus bursting with energy and enjoying a ravenous appetite, I unpacked my trusty wok and prepared a satisfying repast of prawns. It was they that went down under in the end and thankfully not my good self.

SERVES 4

450g/1lb raw (green) prawns
1 tablespoon vegetable oil
1 tablespoon sesame oil
1 garlic clove, finely chopped
1cm/½in piece of fresh root ginger, finely chopped
1 red chilli pepper, deseeded and finely chopped
1 bunch of spring onions, trimmed and sliced
1 large carrot, cut into matchsticks
2 tablespoons coriander root, finely chopped (optional)
salt and freshly ground black pepper
2 tablespoons black bean sauce
coriander leaves or parsley, to garnish

Shell the prawns, leaving the tails intact, and remove the black intestinal vein that runs down the back. In a large frying pan or wok, heat together the oils and sizzle the prawns for about 30 seconds, stirring constantly. Add the garlic, ginger and chilli and stir-fry for a further 30 seconds or so.

Throw in the spring onions and carrot, stir for about 1 minute, then add the chopped coriander root, if using. Season with a little salt and pepper and stir through the black bean sauce. Dish out on to warmed serving plates. Drizzle over a little more black bean sauce and garnish with coriander or parsley. You can't beat plain boiled rice to accompany this.

CHICKEN AND GAME

CHICKEN ROASTED WITH GARLIC

If you do this dish properly, you will get a sweet stuffing of almost puréed creamy garlic and the contrasting crunchy texture and caramelized taste of the whole cloves roasted in the pan. Just pick them up with your fingers and munch the cloves whole – they're truly delicious. What a way to feast on those beautiful violet-tinted bulbs. And you do really need lots of garlic.

SERVES 4

1 x 1.35kg/3lb free-range
   chicken
salt and freshly ground black
   pepper
juice of 1 lemon
900g/2lb plump garlic cloves,
   half in their skins, half peeled

1 bay leaf
1 thyme sprig
olive oil
1 wine-glass of dry white wine

Season the chicken inside and out with salt and pepper, and squeeze the lemon juice inside and over the skin. Stuff the bird with 450g/1lb peeled garlic, the bay leaf and the thyme.

Brown the chicken in olive oil in a frying pan, then transfer it to a roasting tin, breast down. Pop into the oven preheated to 190°C/375°F/gas mark 5 for about 30 minutes, or until the bird takes colour. Add the remaining unpeeled garlic and 1–2 tablespoons of olive oil to the tin, turn the chicken on to its back, baste and continue roasting for approximately 1 hour. (Remember that it will take a little longer than usual to cook because of the stuffing.)

When the bird is cooked, transfer it with the roasted unpeeled garlic cloves to a warmed serving dish. Add the wine to the juices in the roasting tin. Bubble for a moment or two, season to taste with salt and pepper and strain over the dish.

CHICKEN WITH RED PEPPERS

This dish traditionally comes from Aragon in north-east Spain, an arid but dramatic and vividly coloured province. Great battles were fought there with the Moors in the Middle Ages. Anyway, this is not a history lesson, but an introduction to a delicious recipe for what some might call the ubiquitous chicken, to be found all over Spain. But what makes it taste so good are the sweet, sun-ripened peppers and tomatoes and first-class olive oil.

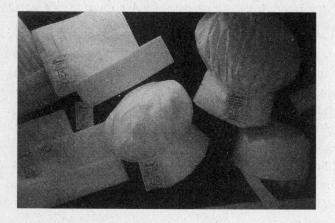

SERVES 4–6

4 tablespoons olive oil
1 x 1.5kg/3½lb free-range
    chicken, jointed into small
    pieces
3–4 garlic cloves, roughly
    crushed
1 onion, chopped
75g/3oz serrano ham or lean
    bacon, diced
2–3 red peppers, cored,
    deseeded and sliced into
    1.25cm/½in wide strips

450g/1lb tomatoes, skinned,
    deseeded and chopped or
    1 x 400g/14oz can of
    chopped tomatoes, drained
1 thyme sprig
1 bay leaf
salt and freshly ground black
    pepper
chopped parsley or coriander,
    to garnish

Heat the oil in a large shallow casserole or heavy, lidded pan. Fry together the chicken pieces, garlic and onion for about 3–5 minutes until they begin to turn golden, then push them to one side of the pan. Add the ham or bacon and peppers and fry these for a minute or so until the peppers soften slightly, then stir everything together. Stand back and admire the brilliant colours.

Stir in the tomatoes, thyme and bay leaf, pop on the lid and simmer over a low heat for about 1½ hours until the chicken is tender and the sauce well reduced. Season to taste with salt and pepper. Remove the bay leaf. Serve garnished with a sprinkling of parsley or coriander, with rice or mashed potatoes.

CHICKEN, CATALAN-STYLE

This is a dish that owes its origins to North Africa and the Middle East where fruit and nuts are often cooked with meat and fowl. It is not a dish easily found in restaurants except perhaps at a restaurant called Casa Irena high in the Pyrenees. After I cooked it there, they promised to put it on the menu – even though it is a very Spanish dish.

SERVES 4

6 tablespoons olive oil
1 x 1.35kg/3lb free-range
   chicken, jointed into quarters
1 onion, chopped
6 ripe tomatoes, finely chopped
250ml/8fl oz chicken stock
100g/4oz stoned prunes

75g/3oz raisins or sultanas
50g/2oz pine nuts
25g/1oz almonds, roasted
2 Rich Tea biscuits, crushed
1 wine-glass of dry white wine
salt and freshly ground black
   pepper

Heat half the oil in a frying pan and pop in the chicken pieces. Fry them, turning over from time to time, for about 10–15 minutes until golden.

Meanwhile, heat the remaining oil in a large saucepan and sauté the onion for about 10 minutes until softened. Stir in the tomatoes and cook gently for 30 minutes, then pour in the stock. Bring up to the boil, then bubble together for about 20 minutes.

Go back to the frying pan and push the chicken joints to one side, then add the prunes, raisins or sultanas and pine nuts. Sizzle together for about 3–4 minutes. Now strain in the onion and tomato sauce through a sieve. Lower the heat and simmer the lot for about 40 minutes.

Just before the end of cooking time, you need to make up a rather interesting paste with the almonds, biscuits and wine. This is called a *picada* in Spain, or a *pomade* in France, and it is used for thickening and flavouring. Grind down the nuts and biscuits, either with a mortar and pestle or in a grinder. Then mix them with the wine and stir into the other ingredients.

Heat everything together for a few moments, check the seasoning, then serve with something simple, like mashed or sauté potatoes.

TRADITIONAL PAELLA

Paella takes its name from the shallow-sided, two-handled fry-ing pan in which it is cooked. In former times the paellas were made from earthenware, but steel ones are more common these days. You will need one at least 24 inches in diameter to make enough for four to six people.

Spanish restaurants have paellas up to 8 feet in diameter. The very biggest one I ever saw was in Benidorm; it must have been 30 feet in diameter, certainly large enough to feed 1,500 people. It was absolutely fascinating to watch five or six cooks literally shovelling rice into this monster pan and throwing in buckets of tomatoes and snails and bucket after bucket of chopped rabbit and chicken. It was just a little party Benidorm puts on once or twice a year to cheer up the visitors. It certainly cheered us up.

Depending on what part of Spain you are in, you will either find meat- or fish-based paellas, or indeed both. Paellas, by the way, are usually eaten for lunch. The recipe I include here is a typical Valencian one made from rabbit, chicken or both, but in other areas they may well add mussels, shrimps, prawns and clams. It is also a question of expense. Snails are often added to the Valencian paella – which doesn't have fish by the way. It is up to you whether or not you use snails.

But whether it is a meat or fish paella, there will always be some kind of vegetable in it, normally fresh peas or beans or dried but cooked beans. Its unique flavour comes from the saffron that is added. Cheapskate cooks pop in turmeric but that only serves to colour it, barely flavouring it in the authentic way.

It was the Arabs who introduced rice to Spain. If they hadn't, I suppose paella wouldn't have been invented. Incidentally, Spain is one of the largest producers of rice in Europe, and the best paellas are made from short-grain rice that has been well-washed and strained before using. A good paella is cooked so that the bottom of the rice forms a crust, not burnt but golden and crunchy. In modern Spain paellas range from pre-prepared, individually frozen portions to mountains of rice with about one prawn or two peas in it to, happily more often than not, a steaming mountain of aromatic rice, meat and vegetables, lovingly cooked. A truly great feast.

SERVES 4-6

1.25–1.5kg/3–3½lb chicken or rabbit, or both, jointed into small pieces

salt and freshly ground black pepper

6 tablespoons olive oil

2 garlic cloves, finely chopped

175g/6oz shelled peas

225g/8oz green beans, runner or French, chopped into 2.5cm/1in pieces, or cooked broad beans or cooked white haricot beans, or all three

4 large tomatoes, peeled and chopped

1 tablespoon paprika

450g/1lb short-grain rice

a few strands of saffron

1.2 litres/2 pints chicken stock

12 snails, cleaned (optional)

3 or 4 large prawns per person

2 lemons, cut into wedges, to garnish

PAELLA *continued*

Season the chicken or rabbit with some salt and pepper. Heat up the oil in a large paella or frying pan, add the chicken or rabbit and sauté for about 10 minutes, turning frequently. Add the garlic, peas, beans and tomatoes. Sprinkle in the paprika, add the rice, saffron and stock and bring to the boil. Add the snails, if using, reduce the heat and bubble gently for about 30 minutes, then add the prawns. When the rice is cooked and the liquid has been absorbed, take the pan off the heat, cover and leave to stand for 5 minutes – this will fluff up the rice. Garnish with lemon wedges and serve with a decent bottle of wine.

FLOYD'S SUNSHINE CHICKEN

This sunny, fruity dish, made with plumptious little raisins, juicy pineapples and fresh limes, celebrates my impression of Florida as a place of plenty – and since I made it on the day that Salvador Dali died, I was inspired to do a little painting on a plate.

SERVES 4

juice of 6–8 limes
1 garlic clove, crushed
salt and freshly ground black pepper
4 boneless free-range chicken breasts
plain flour for dusting
cornmeal for dusting
25g/1oz butter
a dash of rum
1 celery stick, diced

2 tomatoes, skinned, quartered and deseeded
150g/5oz fresh pineapple, cubed
a good dash of Budweiser beer
1 tablespoon raisins, to garnish
TO SERVE:
wild, brown and white rice
a knob of butter
a good pinch of curry powder
a good pinch of saffron powder

Combine the lime juice, garlic and a pinch of salt and marinate the chicken in the mixture for about 2 hours. Drain the chicken, reserving the marinade. Mix together roughly equal quantities of flour and cornmeal, season with salt and pepper and dip the chicken in the mixture to coat thoroughly. Heat the butter in a frying pan and fry the chicken breasts until brown. Flame the chicken with rum. Add the celery, tomatoes, reserved marinade, pineapple cubes and Budweiser. Bubble gently for 20 minutes until the chicken is cooked.

Meanwhile, boil the rice in water to which you have added the butter, curry powder and saffron. Drain, fork up and serve with the chicken, which you have garnished with the raisins.

JAMBALAYA

This Cajun risotto is highly esteemed way down 'yonder in New Orleans. It was introduced by the Spanish and immortalized in song by the great Fats Domino: 'Jambalay, crawfish pie and filé gumbo . . . son of a gun we'll have some fun in the bayou . . .' The night I cooked it in the bayou for a few friends, the film crew and an authentic Cajun band, I was mortified that we had to teach them the words of the song. Under a full Cajun moon and emboldened by a little Louisiana 'moonshine,' I foolishly took the stage and attempted to sing. Happily for my guests, my cooking is more than somewhat better than my singing! (A one, two, three . . .)

SERVES 6

25ml/1fl oz oil

350g/12oz spicy sausage (such as chorizo), sliced

6 free-range chicken breasts, boned and cut into small pieces

salt and freshly ground black pepper

150g/5oz onions, chopped

4 celery sticks, chopped

225g/8oz green peppers, cored, deseeded and chopped

½ tablespoon chopped garlic

750ml/1¼ pints chicken stock

cayenne pepper

1 bouquet garni

400g/14oz white long-grain rice

150g/5oz spring onions, chopped

Heat the oil in a large, heavy saucepan and add the sausage. Season the chicken with salt and pepper and add to the pan. Fry together until browned, then add the 'trinity' of onions, celery and green peppers together with the garlic. Cover with the stock, season to taste with salt and cayenne pepper and add the bouquet garni. Bring to the boil and add the rice. Cover tightly and simmer for 10 minutes. Turn off the heat and leave for 20 minutes to allow the rice to finish cooking. Remove the bouquet garni. Serve garnished with the spring onions.

CHICKEN CURRY WITH COCONUT CREAM AND SWEET POTATOES

I had great fun cooking this mild and slightly sweet curry on the roof of a boat, drifting up and down the river in Saigon. It seems completely mad to cook things on the roof of a boat when you can do it in a perfectly good kitchen, but that's what filming is all about and that's what I do for a living – and I'm not complaining!

SERVES 4

2 tablespoons groundnut oil
1 onion, minced or grated
1 teaspoon minced garlic
1 blade of lemon grass, finely chopped
2 teaspoons mild curry powder
1 teaspoon ground turmeric
2 teaspoons crushed dried red chilli peppers
450g/1lb skinned free-range chicken breast fillets, cubed

about 150ml/5fl oz chicken stock
225ml/8fl oz coconut cream
450g/1lb sweet potato or pumpkin, cubed and deep-fried
salt and freshly ground black pepper
1 teaspoon sugar
red chilli peppers, deseeded and sliced, to garnish

Heat the oil in a large pan or wok and cook the onion and garlic until softened. Add the lemon grass, curry powder, turmeric and dried red chilli peppers. Cook for 2–3 minutes. Add the chicken pieces and coat well with the spices. Pour in enough stock to cover, then simmer until well-reduced. Add the coconut cream and cook for about 20 minutes until the chicken is tender. If you are using a wok, cook over a low heat and keep an eye on it, stirring from time to time. Add the potato or pumpkin cubes approximately 10 minutes before the end of the cooking time. Season to taste with salt, pepper and sugar.

Garnish with slices of fresh red chilli pepper and serve with warm crispy bread or a side dish of stir-fried matchstick courgettes sprinkled with sesame seeds.

BISHOP'S CHICKEN CURRY

While filming in Western Australia, I met the Bishop, whose diocese is about the size of France, Italy, Spain and Germany. Although advanced in years, he flew his own plane; the only practical way to visit his far-flung flock. Anyway, I cooked him this curry and because fresh coconuts were easily available I used fresh coconut milk, but tinned is perfectly fine.

SERVES 4

50g/2oz ghee or clarified butter
2 onions, thinly sliced
1 garlic clove, crushed
1cm/½in piece of fresh root
  ginger, finely chopped
1 red chilli pepper, deseeded and
  finely chopped
2 tablespoons red or green curry
  paste
1 tablespoon ground coriander

½ teaspoon ground turmeric
450g/1lb lean free-range
  chicken, cut into cubes
1 lemon, sliced into little, thin
  slivers
4 tomatoes, skinned and
  chopped
450ml/¾ pint coconut milk
salt and freshly ground black
  pepper

Heat the ghee or clarified butter in a large pan and fry the onions and garlic for about 2–3 minutes. Stir in the ginger and chilli, then add the curry paste, coriander and turmeric and cook gently for 2 minutes. Add the chicken and cook for 2 more minutes, stirring constantly, until the meat is well coated with the spices. Now add the lemon slivers, tomatoes and coconut milk, reheat gently until just bubbling, then cover and simmer for about 1 hour. Season to taste with salt and pepper. Serve with poppadoms, chutney, Cucumber Raita and plain rice.

CUCUMBER RAITA

½ cucumber, peeled and thinly
   sliced
1 teaspoon salt

150ml/5fl oz natural yoghurt
fresh coriander leaves or
   parsley, to garnish

Spread out the cucumber slices and sprinkle with the salt, then leave for 20 minutes or so. Rinse in a colander and drain well, then pat dry with kitchen paper. Put into a serving dish and stir in the yoghurt. Garnish with coriander leaves or parsley.

STUFFED SPRING CHICKENS WITH RED FRUIT SAUCE

SERVES 4

4 x 450g/1lb poussins
salt and freshly ground black
    pepper

FOR THE STUFFING:
100g/4oz fresh white
    breadcrumbs
50g/2oz wheatgerm
50g/2oz celery heart, finely diced
100ml/4fl oz chicken stock
1 tablespoon grated lemon zest
1 tablespoon chopped parsley
1 teaspoon sugar
1 garlic clove, finely chopped
100g/4oz butter, melted

FOR THE SAUCE:
300g/10oz redcurrant jelly
75g/3oz sultanas
50g/2oz butter
a dash of lemon juice
a large pinch of ground
    cinnamon

Mix together all the ingredients for the stuffing, using three-quarters of the butter, in a large bowl. Wipe the birds and season them inside and out with the salt and pepper. Stuff them with the prepared mixture, tucking in the loose bits of skin neatly. Brush the chickens with the remaining melted butter and place them on a wire rack in a roasting tin. Roast in the oven preheated to 220°C/425°F/gas mark 7 for about 20–30 minutes, or until golden-brown.

Meanwhile, prepare the sauce. Put all the ingredients into a pan and cook gently for about 10 minutes, stirring occasionally to mix well. When the chickens are almost cooked, brush them generously all over with the sauce. Return to the oven and roast and baste for 15 more minutes.

Arrange the poussins on warmed serving plates. Heat the remaining sauce, add to it any juices from the roasting tin and hand it round separately.

CHICKEN WITH LEMON GRASS

This is another refreshing, tangy dish from Vietnam. Just one word of warning: take care not to burn the sugar.

SERVES 4

900g/2lb free-range chicken breast fillets, skinned and cubed

2 tablespoons fish sauce

2 teaspoons finely chopped garlic

3 tablespoons white sugar

1 blade of lemon grass, finely chopped

1 teaspoon freshly ground black pepper

2 tablespoons groundnut oil

slivers of deseeded red chilli pepper

Marinate the chicken in the fish sauce, garlic, 1 tablespoon of the sugar, the lemon grass and pepper for 30 minutes.

Heat the oil in a large, lidded pan and sauté the chicken until golden. Lower the heat, cover and simmer for about 20 minutes until the chicken is tender. Keep hot.

Meanwhile, caramelize the remaining sugar by heating it over a medium heat in a small pan. Don't take your eyes off it as it turns liquid and bubbly and as soon as it becomes golden-brown, take it off the heat. Stir in the slivers of chilli and mix them into the chicken. Serve with rice.

SOUTHERN FRIED CHICKEN

As an alternative to gravy, you could serve this chicken with my Memphis Sauce (see the following recipe).

SERVES 4

plain flour for dusting
salt and freshly ground black
   pepper
2 eggs, beaten
a little milk
1 x 1.35kg/3lb free-range
   chicken, jointed
oil for frying

FOR THE GRAVY:
a little plain flour
salt and freshly ground black
   pepper

Season the flour with salt and pepper and combine the eggs and milk. Dust the chicken pieces with the seasoned flour and then dip into the eggwash. In a large frying pan heat about 1cm/½in oil and fry the chicken for about 10–15 minutes, gently to begin with, raising the temperature until it is as brown as desired and cooked through. Remove from the pan and keep warm.

To make the gravy, add a little flour to the fat in the pan and brown slowly. Add cold water, stirring, until the gravy is of the required thickness, and season to taste with salt and pepper. Simmer for a few minutes, then pour over the chicken.

FLOYD'S MEMPHIS SAUCE

Tampering with Southern Fried Chicken can be a dangerous thing in Tennessee, where it is practically a national institution. Traditionally it is served dry, which, I think, is a bit boring. I decided to take my life in my hands and go one step further, so I invented this bacon-flavoured little number with sweetcorn and some crunchy spring onions to counteract the creaminess.

SERVES 4

butter
25g/1oz smoked bacon, diced
2 shallots, finely chopped
1 tablespoon finely diced red
  pepper
1 tablespoon finely diced green
  pepper
2 tablespoons sweetcorn
chicken stock
American or other mild
  mustard
paprika or chilli powder
a knob of butter
Jack Daniels bourbon
a little double cream
salt and freshly ground black
  pepper
chopped spring onions, to
  garnish

Melt a little butter in a pan and add the bacon. Add the shallots, peppers and sweetcorn. Pour in some stock. Turn up the heat and let the sauce bubble for 3–4 minutes. Add a little mustard, a dash of paprika or chilli powder and the butter, plus a little Jack Daniels bourbon to taste. If the sauce tastes bitter, bubble up again to evaporate the alcohol and add a little more butter if necessary. Stir in a little cream, season with salt and pepper, garnish with chopped spring onions and serve instead of gravy with Southern Fried Chicken (see preceding recipe).

DUCK SALAD WITH HOT AND SOUR DRESSING

Do try this creation – it is truly a palate-blowing experience. Each time I return to Koh Samui in Thailand it is the first meal I have that cures the fatigue and jetlag of the flight.

SERVES 4

4 duck breast fillets, roasted or grilled and thinly sliced
fresh crisp lettuce leaves
2 shallots, thinly sliced
4 spring onions, finely chopped
matchstick batons of cucumber and celery (optional)
3 tablespoons fish sauce
1–2 tablespoons lime juice
2 garlic cloves, crushed or finely chopped

1 red and 1 green chilli pepper, deseeded and very finely chopped
1 teaspoon palm or demerara sugar

FOR THE GARNISH:
chilli pepper, sliced and deseeded
spring onions, chopped
chopped roasted peanuts (optional)

Arrange the slices of duck on a bed of lettuce on a serving dish. Sprinkle over the shallots, spring onions and cucumber and celery, if you want.

To make the dressing, put the fish sauce, lime juice, garlic, chillies and sugar into a small pan, and heat through gently. The actual amount of ingredients is just a guide and you can experiment until it is to your liking. Pour the warm dressing over the salad and garnish with the chilli, spring onions and peanuts, if using.

FLOYD'S THAI SPICY DUCK

I am head over heels in love with Thailand. I love the people, its food and its serenity. There is an expression in Thailand: 'one smile makes two'. Somehow that happy, loving attitude comes through in the food. It is spicy, it is fragrant, it is sexy but it is loving and for a real feel of Thailand's food this duck curry (you can use chicken, pork or beef) is a perfect example of everything that is good in this world.

SERVES 2

1 tablespoon sesame oil (toasted sesame oil has the best flavour)

2 teaspoons finely chopped lemon grass

2 garlic cloves, finely chopped

1 tablespoon finely chopped fresh root ginger

1 lime leaf, finely shredded

2 teaspoons red curry paste

2 tablespoons coconut milk

225g/8oz roast duck, diced

25g/1oz spring onions, sliced

25g/1oz red pepper, sliced

25g/1oz cucumber or green beans, sliced

1 tomato, diced

25g/1oz cooking apple or mango, cut into large dice

1 tablespoon chopped coriander

1 tablespoon chopped basil

FOR THE COCONUT RICE:

100g/4oz Thai fragrant rice

100ml/4fl oz water

4 tablespoons coconut milk

salt and freshly ground black pepper

First prepare the coconut rice. Rinse the rice two or three times, then drain well. Put it in a large saucepan and add the water and coconut milk. Season with a little salt and pepper. Cover and cook for about 20–25 minutes until tender.

When the rice is almost cooked, heat the oil in a wok or large frying pan. Add the lemon grass, garlic, ginger and lime leaf and stir-fry for a few seconds. Add the red curry paste, fry for a few seconds, then blend in the coconut milk. Add the duck, spring onions and red pepper. Stir-fry for 2–3 minutes, then add the cucumber or green beans, tomato and apple or mango and stir-fry for a few more seconds. Stir through half the herbs and serve at once with the rice. Sprinkle with the remaining herbs.

RABBIT WITH PEARS AND TURNIPS

I have included this dish because of the fascinating combination
of ingredients, namely rabbit and pears. A simple rabbit stew
with carrots, onions and turnips – little baby ones, nicely peeled
– cooked in stock would be a nice English way to prepare this.
But the addition of pears and a drop of white wine lifts it out of
the ordinary and into the exotic and amusing. This recipe
is so typical of real Spanish country food, but hard to find in
restaurants.

SERVES 4

1 x 1.35kg/3lb rabbit
2 tablespoons plain flour
salt and freshly ground black
   pepper
250ml/8fl oz olive oil
½ wine-glass of brandy
1 wine-glass of dry white wine
250ml/8fl oz chicken or rabbit
   stock or water
1 large onion, chopped
2 garlic cloves, chopped

1 large carrot, roughly chopped
4 turnips, roughly chopped
1 leek, sliced
2 ripe tomatoes, skinned and
   chopped
1 small bundle of fresh herbs
   such as thyme, rosemary,
   parsley and a bay leaf
4 large pears, unpeeled, cored
   and quartered

Roll the rabbit pieces in the flour seasoned with salt and pepper. Heat half the oil in a large flameproof casserole and fry the rabbit for about 10 minutes until golden-brown. Pour in the brandy and set fire to it with a match. When the flames have died down, pour in the wine and stock or water. Bubble away gently while you carry on in another pan.

Heat the remaining oil and fry the onion, garlic, carrot, turnips and leek for about 8–10 minutes until soft, then pop in the tomatoes and bouquet garni. Tip this lot over the rabbit and carry on cooking, adding more liquid as needed, until the rabbit is really tender – about 1¼ hours should be fine. Ten minutes before serving, sauté the pears in olive oil and add to the dish.

GUINEA FOWL WITH PEACHES

I've cooked this one more times than I care to remember but on my first ever television performance I had to use a frozen bird and forgot to remove the plastic bag of giblets before roasting it. I flamboyantly cut it in half in front of millions of people and whoops there was the plastic sack.

The television company did not think it very funny and sacked me.

SERVES 4

1 x 900g/2lb guinea fowl
salt and freshly ground black
  pepper
chopped thyme
chopped basil
juice of 1 lemon
75g/3oz butter

4 ripe peaches, halved
1 wine-glass of dry white wine
1 measure of brandy or peach
  liqueur
about 4 tablespoons chicken
  stock

Wipe the bird and season it inside and out with salt, pepper, thyme and basil. Rub with lemon juice and butter and place in a roasting tin, breast side down. Roast in the oven preheated to 220°C/425°F/gas mark 7 for 15 minutes.

Add the peaches and wine and cook for 15 more minutes, breast side up, basting frequently. When the skin is brown and the flesh moist (it must not be overcooked), remove the bird and joint it. Place with the peaches on a warmed serving dish, pour over the brandy or peach liqueur and flame.

Meanwhile, bubble the juices in the roasting tin over a high direct heat until reduced by half. Then add the stock plus the juices that have oozed out from the flamed bird on the serving dish. There is not much sauce but it is delicious so don't cook it away. Strain over the guinea fowl and serve immediately.

POT ROASTED PIGEONS

Pigeons are notoriously tough so I would take the trouble and money to order imported pigeons from a good game dealer. They need to be plump, well rounded and with a smooth skin. Reject birds with a prominent breast bone and concave breasts.

SERVES 4

4 pigeons

a handful of fresh sage

salt and freshly ground black pepper

4 tablespoons olive oil

1 onion, finely chopped

1 celery stick, finely chopped

2 garlic cloves, finely chopped

600ml/1 pint pigeon, chicken or game stock

2 wine-glasses of Chianti Classico

2 tablespoons tomato purée

100g/4oz pigeon or chicken livers, finely chopped

225g/8oz Arborio (short-grain) rice

50g/2oz butter

50g/2oz hard sheep's cheese, such as Pecorino Romano or Sardo

Stuff the pigeons with the sage and season all over with salt and pepper. Heat the oil in a large flameproof casserole and brown the birds. Next add the onion. Cook for a couple of minutes, then stir in the celery and garlic. Add most of the stock, the wine, tomato purée and pigeon or chicken livers. Allow the wine to evaporate a little, then cover and simmer over a low heat for about 45 minutes until the birds are tender.

Transfer the pigeons to another cooking pot and add a couple of spoonfuls of the sauce. Cover and simmer very gently to keep warm. Stir the rice into the remaining sauce and cook for about 12–15 minutes until the liquid has been absorbed. Add a little more stock if necessary. The rice should be moist and tender, but very slightly nutty.

Stir the butter into the rice and let it melt, then add the cheese. Heap this risotto on to warmed serving plates and place the pigeons on top. Pour over the sauce.

AUTUMN BAROSSA PHEASANT

A simple dish cooked in the Barossa valley in Oz at a place called the Pheasant Farm with Maggie Beer who had loads of beetroot in the garden and jars of superb quince preserve in her larder . . . and a cellar full of delicious Barossa red.

SERVES 4

100g/4oz butter
1 pheasant
450g/1lb fresh baby beetroot, peeled and parboiled for 10 minutes, then halved or quartered depending on size
6 shallots, finely chopped
25g/1oz plain flour
12 juniper berries, crushed
a dash of strong Australian red wine

3 tablespoons chicken or pheasant stock
salt and freshly ground black pepper
350g/12oz wild mushrooms, preferably ceps, or field mushrooms
fresh noodles or pasta, to serve
quince jelly or preserve

Rub half the butter over the pheasant and roast the bird, breast-side down, in a roasting tin in the oven preheated to 200°C/400°F/gas mark 6 for about 30 minutes. Remove from the oven, put the parboiled beets round the bird so that they can roast like little potatoes and then roast for 30–40 minutes more until tender.

Strain about 150ml/5fl oz pheasant stock from the roasting tin and return the pheasant, with the beets, to a low oven to keep warm. Melt half the remaining butter in a pan and fry the shallots for 4–5 minutes until golden. Remove from the heat and stir in the flour, then cook over a low heat for 1 minute. Add the pheasant stock, crushed juniper berries, wine and chicken stock and bring to the boil, stirring constantly. Boil away until reduced by half: you should now have a thick, rich gravy. Season to taste with salt and pepper and strain into a sauceboat.

Melt the remaining butter in a frying pan and sauté the ceps or field mushrooms for 3–4 minutes. Carve or joint the pheasant and serve with the roast beets, mushrooms and rich gravy, with a bowl of buttered noodles or the pasta of your choice, and quince jelly or preserve.

PARTRIDGE IN CHOCOLATE, TOLEDO-STYLE

Chocolate has been used in Spanish cooking since the discovery of the Americas; I discovered it when I was filming *Floyd on Spain* and had the great pleasure of cooking this dish for a Spanish marqués. The Marqués de Griñón no less, who has an estate 50 kilometres or so west of Toledo, which is a magnificent town that has been pretty much ruined by souvenir shops selling imitation El Cid swords.

Like every self-respecting country estate, this one has a chapel attached to the house for the occasional family service. I don't think you can say you have really made it until you own a church or chapel. The house is surrounded by acres of carefully tended vines and is found at the end of a 400-yard drive, the borders of which are thick with wild flowers, thyme and laven-der, creating the appropriately rich scent that you would expect to inhale as you wandered around the estate of a marqués with your 12-bore, rustic retainer and couple of gun dogs putting up the odd partridge of an early morning.

Add to that a thriving and innovative wine business, probably a small palace in Madrid, a beautiful wife and a British racing green Daimler, a wardrobe of well-cut clothes and hand-made shoes and you too would be extremely happy.

I have to say that the Marqués de Griñón – who happened to be the President of the Spanish Gastronomic Society, which made me a bit nervous having to cook for him, I can tell you – is an absolutely smashing chap, urbane, charming, hospitable and friendly. And as only a real gentleman can, he puts you at ease with generous glasses of wine, slivers of fine cheese and excellent ham. And what really made me warm to him was that he pronounced my finished dish a triumph. Hope you like it too!

SERVES 4

2–4 partridges, cleaned

salt and freshly ground black pepper

3 tablespoons olive oil

1 medium onion, chopped

2 garlic cloves, finely chopped

1 tablespoon plain flour

1 tablespoon red or white wine vinegar

225ml/8fl oz chicken or game stock

1 wine-glass of dry white wine

2 bay leaves

2 cloves

2–3 tablespoons grated dark chocolate (bitter is best)

Season the birds with salt and pepper. Heat the oil in a deep, flameproof casserole, add the partridges and fry them for 5 minutes or so to brown them on all sides. Add the onion and garlic and cook for 2–3 more minutes until they soften.

Now stir in the flour and mix well to make a roux, then add the vinegar, stock, wine, bay leaves and cloves. Bring up to the boil and season with a little more salt and pepper.

Cover the pot and leave to simmer for about 30–40 minutes, or until the birds are tender. Stir in the grated chocolate, mixing it in well, cover and cook for 15 more minutes. Transfer the birds to a warmed serving dish and strain the sauce through a fine sieve over them.

This tastes good with some plain boiled potatoes and a green salad.

POT ROAST HAUNCH OF VENISON

Jimmy MacNab is the archetypal Scot – a cheerful, kilt-wearing, (occasional) whisky-drinking giant of a man who loves his food and a good yarn at The Creggans Hotel in Stachur (proprietors Sir Fitzroy and Lady Maclean. Some say Sir Fitzroy was the model of Fleming's James Bond). When Jimmy cooks he does so with gusto, and this old-fashioned recipe is superb for a big dinner party or a Christmas celebration.

SERVES 8 – 10

2 onions	whole cloves
3 carrots	225ml/8fl oz olive oil
2 parsnips	100g/4oz soft light brown sugar
2 turnips	dried mixed herbs
1 head of celery	chopped thyme, rosemary and
2 apples	mint
1 x 4.5kg/10lb haunch of	1½ bottles of red wine
venison	

Finely chop the vegetables and apples, place in a large ovenproof pot, and set the venison on top. Make several incisions in the top of the meat, inserting cloves as you go. Rub the oil and sugar into the meat, sprinkle over some mixed herbs and the thyme, rosemary and mint. Pour the wine into the pot and leave to marinate in a cool place for 4 days, turning occasionally.

When ready to cook, cover the pot with foil and cook in a preheated oven (180°C/350°F/gas mark 4) for about 3½ hours (allow 20 minutes' cooking time for each 450g/1lb).

MEAT

STUFFED BEEF OLIVES

This is a classic example of the French people's ability to make tasty, satisfying, yet economical dishes. And you don't have to be a genius to prepare and cook this one.

SERVES 6

300g/10oz lean pork, minced
a small handful of parsley, chopped
3 garlic cloves, minced
salt and freshly ground black pepper
900g/2lb stewing beef, cut into slices, beaten out as thin as possible

2 tablespoons olive oil
675g/1½lb tomatoes, skinned, deseeded and chopped
2 tablespoons Cognac
2 tablespoons plain flour
1 wine-glass of red wine
chopped thyme

Mix the pork, parsley, 1 garlic clove, salt and pepper together and distribute evenly between the slices of beef. Roll up and tie with string or secure with a wooden cocktail stick.

Fry the remaining garlic in the oil with half the tomatoes in a large saucepan or deep frying pan. Add the meat parcels and brown carefully. Flame with the Cognac and sprinkle with the flour. Mix the flour well with the juices and cook for a minute or two before adding the wine, the remaining tomatoes, thyme, salt and pepper, and stir. Cover and simmer gently for 2 hours.

BEEF AND MUSHROOMS
IN RUBESCO WINE

Autumn in Umbria. The time of the year for the wine harvest
and that gradual shift from warm sunny days to cool nights and
crisp misty mornings. The time of hard work and anxiety to
gather the harvest before the weather breaks and the time of
great excitement because the Italians are potty about gathering
wild mushrooms.

This dish is perfectly suited to autumn. Certainly, the head-
man from the Torgiano vineyards thought it splendid. You
could serve it with freshly boiled pasta (fresh pasta is easily available these days), or with sauté potatoes or rice.

SERVES 4

3–4 tablespoons olive oil
675g/1½lb chump or braising
   steak, cut into large chunks
salt and freshly ground black
   pepper
450ml/¾ pint Rubesco wine or
   other good-quality Italian red
   wine
300ml/½ pint Fresh Tomato Sauce
   (see page 157), or passata or
   other prepared tomato sauce
a few sage and parsley sprigs

2–3 garlic cloves, unpeeled
about 50g/2oz fat cut from
   Parma ham, diced into
   small cubes
350g/12oz wild mushrooms or
   good-flavoured mushrooms
   such as ceps or chestnut
   mushrooms, roughly
   chopped
chopped sage and parsley,
   to garnish

Heat the oil in a large frying pan and add the meat, sealing and browning it over a high heat. Season with salt and pepper. Transfer the meat to a casserole dish, adding a little more oil. Pour in the wine and add the tomato sauce. Pop in the sage, parsley and garlic cloves. Cover and cook over a low heat or in the oven preheated to 180°C/350°F/gas mark 4 for 1½ hours or until the beef is really tender.

Towards the end of cooking time, sauté the fat from the Parma ham to render it down. Add the mushrooms and sauté them briskly for 4–5 minutes. Season with salt and pepper and add a good pinch of chopped sage and parsley. Add to the beef stew, stir well and serve.

PROVENÇAL BEEF STEW

This is a wonderful winter dish that benefits from long, slow cooking. Traditionalists prefer it cooked in the oven in an earthenware pot with the lid sealed with a paste of flour and water to prevent any flavours escaping. It's what Agas are made for! The best one I ever made was cooked in a baker's wood oven after he'd finished the morning's bread – it simply sat in the dying embers for a couple of hours.

SERVES 6

1.8kg/4lb good stewing beef, cut into chunks

225g/8oz smoked streaky bacon, finely diced

oil

2 garlic cloves, chopped

2 tablespoons Cognac

3 tablespoons plain flour

1 wine-glass of good red wine

2 tablespoons red wine vinegar

FOR THE MARINADE:

4 wine-glasses of good red wine

2 tablespoons red wine vinegar

2 tablespoons finely chopped garlic

1 thyme sprig

3 cloves

1 bay leaf

a small handful of parsley, chopped

sea salt and freshly ground black pepper

1 large onion, chopped

Combine the meat with all the marinade ingredients and leave overnight.

Fry the bacon in some of the oil with the garlic. Drain the meat, reserving the marinade, add to the bacon and brown all over. Pour over the warmed Cognac and flame. Sprinkle on the flour and stir well. Pour on the marinade, wine and vinegar. Stir well and cover. Simmer gently for 3 hours, adding water if necessary. The sauce should be rich, thick and spicy, the meat very tender.

Often this dish is served with plain boiled noodles sprinkled with grated cheese and freshly milled black pepper.

BEEF STEW WITH GARLIC
AND PRUNES

On a crisp autumn morning under a clear blue sky I crossed the Spanish Pyrenees in an open-topped car thinking about lunch. I stopped at a roadside tourist restaurant which was busy feeding a huge wedding party on this Sunday morning. I was squeezed into a back room with some locals who had been shooting. They were mopping up big bowls of dark stew with thick wedges of coarse bread. In my impeccable Spanish, pointing simultaneously to my mouth, and to their plates, I conveyed to the waitress that I would have what they had had.

Serves 4–6

2 tablespoons olive oil
900g/2lb stewing beef, cubed,
    with some fat on the meat
at least 6 garlic cloves, peeled
    and roughly chopped
1 onion, chopped
½ teaspoon cornflour
1 wine-glass of dry white wine
175g/6oz tomatoes, skinned
    and chopped

3 cloves
1 large bay leaf
1 teaspoon chopped thyme
1 teaspoon chopped oregano
1 tablespoon chopped parsley
3 large potatoes, cut into
    chunks
225g/8oz prunes, stoned
salt and freshly ground black
    pepper

Heat the oil in a large cooking pot. Chuck in the meat, brown it, and sauté for 25 minutes, keeping the heat on high, then turn it down and add the garlic and onion. Cook for about 4–5 minutes until they soften, stirring all the while.

Mix the cornflour with the wine and add to the meat, stirring well until slightly thickened. Add all the remaining ingredients except the potatoes and prunes and a drop of water or more wine if necessary (though this should be a fairly dry stew). Simmer, covered, for about 1¾ hours, until the meat is tender but not falling apart.

Meanwhile, and when it suits you, parboil the potatoes for 10 minutes. In a separate pan, simmer the prunes in a little water for about 10–12 minutes to swell them up.

When the meat is almost ready, pop the potatoes into the pot and cook for 10 more minutes. Finally, add the drained prunes and cook just long enough to heat them through. This way the prunes keep their distinctive flavour and don't get swallowed up by the stew. Season to taste with salt and pepper.

FILLET OF BEEF WITH STOUT AND OYSTERS

The traditional beef-browned stew in Ireland is often cooked with stout instead of water and a beef, mushroom and oyster stew is a delight. (By the way, brown your meat and onions, add a little flour, a tablespoon of tomato purée, some bay leaves and parsley, salt and pepper, a few mushrooms and simmer in stout until tender.) However, challenged by my great friend, the Irish chef Billy Mackesee, to create an original Floyd Irish dish, I came up with this!

SERVES 4

1 x 450g/1lb piece of beef fillet, trimmed
150ml/5fl oz stout (preferably Murphy's)
150ml/5fl oz strong beef stock
2 shallots, chopped
1 bay leaf

1 teaspoon soft light brown sugar
25g/1oz butter
salt and freshly ground black pepper
16 oysters, removed from shells

Poach the whole piece of beef fillet in a mixture of the stout and stock with the shallots and bay leaf for about 10 minutes (the beef should be rare in the middle). Remove the meat and keep warm.

Add the sugar to the stock mixture and reduce by about one-third; finally whisk in the butter to make the sauce thick and shiny. Season to taste with salt and pepper. Pop the oysters into the sauce for 1 minute and then remove.

Pour the sauce on to white warmed plates, then slice the beef thinly and arrange decoratively on top. Garnish each portion with the poached oysters.

Alternatively, you could garnish the dish with a julienne of carrots and leeks, in which case put a little of this on to each plate and set the oysters on top.

WILD BOAR STEW

Wild boar has a deeper, richer, more gamey flavour than the domestic pig. Generally in Britain wild boar is difficult to obtain and very expensive. However, farmed boar is an acceptable alternative. You can use a leg of pork, but you should increase the marinade time to forty-eight hours as opposed to the twenty-four hours I recommend for wild boar.

Serves 6

1 leg of wild boar, cut into large pieces, or about 1kg/2¼lb leg of pork or venison
1 bottle of decent Italian red wine (I used La Suvera Rango 1988)
2–3 bay leaves
rosemary sprigs
sage sprigs
2–3 garlic cloves
1 carrot, cut into dice
2 red onions, quartered
6 tablespoons olive oil
salt and freshly ground black pepper
300ml/½ pint Fresh Tomato Sauce (see page 159) or passata or other prepared tomato sauce

Put the pieces of meat into a large non-aluminium bowl and pour in three-quarters of the wine. (Keep the rest of the bottle for later.) Add the bay leaves, rosemary, sage, garlic, carrot and onions. Cover and leave in a cool place or refrigerate for 24 hours, to allow the meat to absorb the flavours.

Next day, heat the oil in a large cooking pot. Add the meat

and seal and brown it on all sides over a high heat. Add salt and pepper, then pour in the marinade. Stir in the tomato sauce and add another glass of red wine for good measure. Cover and cook in the oven preheated to 180°C/350°F/gas mark 4 for about 2–2½ hours until the meat is very tender. Fish out the bay leaves.

Serve with vegetables fried in olive oil and peaches simmered in sweet wine and brown sugar.

AMERICAN RIBS

You can use beef ribs, lamb ribs (breast of lamb) or pork ribs. Barbecue cooked ribs are embedded deep in the gastronomic psyche of the American gastronaut. Gastronauts don't regard ribs as junk food, they regard them as fun food and a plate of ribs, washed down with what made Milwaukee famous, is a fun eating experience.

(PS The rockologists among you will know that I refer to a Rod Stewart song with a line that goes 'What's Made Milwaukee Famous [Has Made A Loser Out Of Me]'. He was referring to Schlitz beer.)

SERVES ABOUT 4

1.35kg/3lb beef ribs
50ml/2fl oz oil
1 medium onion, chopped
2 celery sticks
1 garlic clove, crushed
50ml/2fl oz dry white wine
100ml/4fl oz soy sauce

¼ teaspoon chilli powder
¼ teaspoon freshly ground
   black pepper
225g/8oz tomato ketchup
8 carrots, chopped
4 potatoes, chopped

Brown the ribs in the oil in a flameproof casserole. Then mix together all the remaining ingredients and pour over. Bake in the oven preheated to 170°C/325°F/gas mark 3 for 2 hours.

SPIT-ROASTED FILLET OF BEEF WITH CREAM AND PEPPER

SERVES 4

900g/2lb fillet of beef with fat
   still on
2 tablespoons black peppercorns,
   crushed

3 tablespoons oil
salt
150ml/5fl oz double cream
2 tablespoons Cognac

Roll the beef in the peppercorns until all have been firmly lodged into the meat. Paint with some of the oil and sprinkle with salt.

Place a drip tray under the spit to catch the juices and pop the fillet on to the spit. Cook for about 20 minutes.

Just before the meat is cooked, add the cream to the tray under the meat. Pour the Cognac over the meat and let it flame. Remove the beef to a carving tray or board and leave it to rest for a few minutes. Meanwhile, whisk the cream and the juices with a fork, reheat if necessary and pour over the fillet.

THE GASTRONAUT'S HAMBURGER

A good hamburger should taste like the sound of 'Under The Boardwalk', a great Drifters song of the early sixties. Anyone found using frozen hamburgers will lose the status of Honorary Gastronaut that comes free with this book.

SERVES 4

675g/ 1 ½lb beef, finely chopped rather than minced
1 hard-boiled egg, finely chopped
1 onion, finely chopped
1 tablespoon finely chopped chives, parsley and chervil

2 tablespoons olive oil
salt and freshly ground black pepper
1 tablespoon mild French mustard
Barbecue Sauce (see page 162)

Put all the ingredients except the mustard and the barbecue sauce into a bowl, mix very thoroughly and roll into a ball. Now divide the ball into 4 smaller ones of equal size and with the palm of your hand flatten them to the desired thickness.

Before cooking the hamburgers, spread each one with the mustard. To cook, either barbecue gently over hot coals or fry in a little hot fat over a gentle-moderate heat for about 10 minutes or so, depending on the thickness and how well done you like them, turning them half-way through or as needed. Serve with Barbecue Sauce.

PORK KEBABS WITH GREEN PEPPERCORNS

SERVES 4

1 tablespoon green peppercorns

2 tablespoons Cognac

550g/1¼lb boneless pork, cut into 2.5cm/1in cubes

175g/6oz smoked bacon, cut into small cubes

salt

Crush the peppercorns and mix in the Cognac to make a paste. Stir in the pork and bacon cubes and leave to marinate for at least 2 hours.

Thread the pork and bacon on to skewers and cook for about 12 minutes, turning and basting frequently. Season with salt and serve with steamed fragrant rice.

CASTILIAN ROAST LAMB

When you order roast lamb in Spain you are invariably given a whole shoulder or leg from a very young animal. This has been simply seasoned with salt, pepper and garlic, probably placed on a bed of thickly sliced potatoes, onions and whole garlic cloves, liberally soused in olive oil, and roasted in a fiercely hot oven until the meat begins to fall off the bone and the onions and potatoes cook into a golden crunchy-topped pancake.

You could certainly add thickly sliced potatoes and onions and garlic to the roasting tin when you prepare this wonderful aromatic dish.

SERVES 4–6

1 × 1.5kg/3½lb leg of lamb
2 tablespoons olive oil
salt and freshly ground black pepper
1 teaspoon paprika
1 teaspoon chopped oregano
1 teaspoon chopped thyme
4 garlic cloves, cut into slivers
2 teaspoons rosemary leaves
900g/2lb potatoes, sliced
225g/8oz onions, sliced
1 large wine-glass of dry white wine
2 tablespoons white wine vinegar
juice of 1 lemon

Rub the lamb all over with half the oil, then season it with salt and pepper. Mix together the paprika, oregano and thyme and rub this mixture over the surface of the lamb. Let the lamb sit for an hour to absorb the flavours.

Make small slits in the leg of lamb and pop slivers of garlic into them, then rub the lamb with the remaining oil. Scatter over the rosemary.

Sit the lamb on a griddle over the roasting tin with the potato and onion slices and olive oil underneath the meat and roast in the oven preheated to 230°C/450°F/gas mark 8 for 15 minutes. Meanwhile, put the wine, vinegar and lemon juice into a pan and bring to the boil.

Reduce the oven temperature to 190°C/375°F/gas mark 5. Pour about half the liquid over the meat and roast until it is done, basting from time to time with the remaining liquid. The length of cooking time depends on the size of your piece of lamb and how you like it cooked. Allow 15 minutes per 450g/1lb if you like your lamb pink, 25 minutes per 450g/1lb if you want it well done. The Spanish like their meats well done, but that doesn't mean you have to.

The potatoes and onions underneath the meat should be crunchy and juicy.

IRISH STEW

I spend a lot of time in Ireland and am – even if I say it myself – something of an expert on that wondrous concoction of lamb and vegetables known as Irish stew. I have adapted this recipe from the great Irish cook and campaigner for things fresh, local and simple, Myrtle Allen, who is to Ireland's national cookery what Elizabeth David or Jane Grigson were to Britain. Irish stew is a fine dish, it is to be celebrated!

SERVES 4

1–1.35kg/2½–3lb mutton neck chops
4 medium onions
4 medium carrots
600ml/1 pint beef stock or water
salt and freshly ground black pepper
6 potatoes
15g/½oz butter
1 tablespoon snipped chives
1 tablespoon chopped parsley

Cut the excess fat from the chops, shred it and render it down in a heavy flameproof casserole. Toss the meat in the fat until coloured. Cut the onions and carrots into quarters, add to the meat and turn in the fat also. Add the stock or water and season carefully with salt and pepper.

Simmer gently for approximately 2 hours, adding the potatoes halfway through. When the meat is cooked, pour off the cooking liquid, degrease and reheat in another saucepan. Check the seasoning. Swirl in the butter, chives and parsley and pour back over the meat. Finally, sieve one of the potatoes and stir into the stew to thicken it.

LAMB CHOPS WITH MINT

As the first summer swallows swoop into our lives, a strange fever grips the men of our great nation. By some mystic process they are gripped with a conviction that they can cook and create mayhem and madness in their wives' kitchens, a place in which during the winter they have probably spent no time at all. They sally forth into the garden and set about incinerating sausages, chops and burgers. The reason that these barbecues are so often a disaster is because the cook of the day is too impatient to wait for the flames on the charcoal to die down until the cinders are covered with a fine white dust – only then should you place your meat over the fire. End of lecture – here is the recipe.

SERVES 4

8 lamb chops or 4 leg steaks
100ml/4fl oz cider vinegar
100ml/4fl oz water
1 tablespoon soft light brown
   sugar
1 tablespoon black
   peppercorns, finely crushed
a handful of mint, finely
   chopped
1 tablespoon oil

Trim the lamb chops or steaks. Bring the vinegar and water to the boil in a pan. Add the sugar, peppercorns and mint. Boil for 3 more minutes or until the liquid is well-reduced.

Now simply oil the chops. Seal them quickly for 2 minutes on each side on the barbecue or under a hot grill, then paint with mint sauce. Cook for 8–10 more minutes depending on how you like your lamb, turning occasionally and adding more mint sauce. Serve the remaining sauce with the chops.

PORK AND PRAWN STEW

Like the other Vietnamese recipes in this book, this pork and prawn stew is a subtle blend of spices and sweetness. Carefully prepared Vietnamese food has a subtlety of flavour which is outstanding and, dare I say it, more sophisticated and elegant than its Chinese relations.

SERVES 4

450g/1lb pork tenderloin, cut into 2.5cm/1in pieces
2 garlic cloves, finely chopped or minced
3 shallots, finely chopped
3 tablespoons fish sauce
3 spring onions, finely chopped
2 tablespoons groundnut oil
4–6 tablespoons soft light brown sugar

300ml/½ pint coconut water (from 2 fresh coconuts) or diluted tinned coconut cream
225g/8oz raw prawns, peeled and deveined
2 teaspoons finely chopped or minced fresh root ginger
2 red chilli peppers, deseeded and sliced

Marinate the pork with half the garlic, the shallots, 2 tablespoons of the fish sauce and the spring onions for at least 30 minutes.

Heat half the oil in a pan and sprinkle in 2–3 tablespoons of the sugar. Do not heat too quickly and watch it like a hawk. Just as the sugar begins to caramelize and turn a toffee colour, add the marinated pork and stir it into the oil and sugar, coating well. This seals the meat and colours the sauce you are going to make. Cook until the pork has turned a deep golden-brown (coloured by the sugar), then add the coconut water or coconut cream. Simmer gently for about 30 minutes until the stock is reduced and the meat tender.

Meanwhile, marinate the prawns in the remaining fish sauce, ginger and remaining garlic for 15 minutes. Fry the prawns in sugared oil (as for the pork) until they change colour. Add them to the stew shortly before the cooking is complete. Garnish with sliced chilli peppers and serve with steamed rice.

BOILED BACON WITH PEASE PUDDING

This is one of my all time favourite meals. If you don't have time to make a pease pudding, you can boil the bacon with cabbage instead. Just before the bacon is cooked, you chuck in a load of coarsely chopped spring cabbage and then serve it alongside the bacon with lots of salt and freshly milled black pepper, melted butter and masses of lovely mustard. And, of course, My Mum's Parsley Sauce (see page 160). As a boy I often stole into the larder late at night to munch a piece of left-over cold pudding. Yum yum!!

SERVES 4–6

FOR THE PEASE PUDDING:
225g/8oz split peas
salt
25g/1oz butter
1 egg
freshly ground black pepper
a pinch of sugar

FOR THE BACON:
1.35kg/3lb bacon joint,
    forehock or collar
1 bay leaf
a few cloves
1 onion, sliced

Wash the peas and soak in cold water overnight. Drain and tie loosely in a cloth. Place in a pan with a pinch of salt and cover with boiling water. Boil for 2–3 hours until soft.

Meanwhile, put the bacon into a pan with the bay leaf, cloves and onion. Cover with water and boil until cooked, allowing 25 minutes per 450g/1lb, plus 25 minutes.

Rub the peas through a sieve or purée them in a food processor or blender. Add the butter and egg and season to taste with salt, pepper and the sugar. Beat until lightly mixed. Tie up tightly in a floured cloth and boil for 30 more minutes.

Serve the pudding with the strained hot bacon and carrots or swede and parsley sauce (see page 160).

GOULASH OF LAMBS' SWEETBREADS

Ah! The poor sweetbread, reviled by the British population –
those with long memories, that is – who still regard all kinds of
offal as either a penance, illness or poverty, esteemed in Europe
and endangered by the bland grey bureaucrats of the EU.
Sweetbreads simply sautéed in sizzling golden butter, seasoned
with lemon juice and garnished with capers is a French classic.
Here's another from Hungary.

SERVES 4

675g/1½lb lambs' sweetbreads
1 slice of lemon
salt
75g/3oz butter
675g/1½lb Spanish onions,
   thinly sliced
2 teaspoons ground paprika,
   preferably Hungarian –
   the best kind

15g/½oz plain flour
300ml/½ pint chicken stock
freshly ground black pepper
65ml/2½fl oz double cream
1 red pepper, cored, deseeded,
   skinned and shredded

Soak the sweetbreads in cold salted water for several hours to
remove any blood. Drain, place in a pan of cold water and add
a slice of lemon and some salt. Bring slowly to the boil, then
simmer for 1–2 minutes. Drain and rinse well. Press the sweetbreads between two boards or plates and weight down for

about 1 hour. Remove all the fine outer skin and any membrane from the sweetbreads.

Melt 50g/2oz of the butter in a sauté pan, add the onions and allow to soften, uncovered, for about 20 minutes. Remove the onions from the pan. Add the remaining butter and quickly brown the well-drained sweetbreads, then remove from the pan. Reduce the heat, add the paprika, cook for 1–2 minutes and then mix in the flour and stock. Season lightly to taste with salt and pepper and return the sweetbreads to the pan. Cover and simmer very gently for 20–30 minutes until tender.

Just before serving, add the cream and red pepper.

FLOYD'S CHUCK WAGON PORK AND BEANS

SERVES 4–6

175g/6oz dried black beans
½ teaspoon salt
2 bay leaves
½ teaspoon freshly ground
   black pepper
½ teaspoon cumin seeds
½ teaspoon dried oregano
2 tablespoons vegetable oil
675g/1½lb boned pork
   shoulder, cubed

2–3 jalapeño or other chilli
   peppers, chopped
1 onion, chopped
2 garlic cloves, finely chopped
3 tablespoons crushed red chilli
   pepper
2 tablespoons blue cornmeal
   or cornflour
2 tablespoons clear honey

Soak the beans overnight in plenty of cold water. Drain, then boil for 2 hours with the salt, bay leaves, pepper, cumin seeds and oregano. Strain, reserving the liquid, and set aside. Heat the oil in a pan (preferably a cauldron hung over a wood fire, wood mark 3!) and add the pork, jalapeños, onion and garlic. In a bowl mix the red chilli peppers, cornmeal or cornflour and the cooking liquid from the beans to make a kind of cowboy roux. Stir this into the pan. Add the beans and finally the honey. Simmer for about 2 hours. Serve as the sun goes down around an open fire, with a bottle of Kentucky Fried Gentleman and someone playing guitar.

GRILLED CALF'S LIVER

The beauty of this queen of offals is in the simplicity of its cooking. As Jane Grigson once said, 'One of the best ingredients you can afford and do as little as possible with it.' Calf's liver is the perfect proof of this maxim.

SERVES 4

4 x 110g/4oz slices of calf's liver, 1cm/½in thick
salt and freshly ground black pepper

olive oil
lemon wedges

Sprinkle salt over the grill rack and when the barbecue or grill is very hot place the liver slices on the rack and grill for about 45 seconds on each side – the liver should be brown on the outside and a beautiful light pink inside. Sprinkle the cooked liver with pepper and olive oil and garnish with lemon wedges.

OXTAIL STEW

The British Government ought to make Oxtail Stew compulsory in places like Heathrow Airport, and ports of entry, so that people can have at least one decent British meal when they arrive!

Oxtails make the most delicious stews, and they aren't expensive. But as they are fatty, you should cook the stew the day before you want to eat it, then strain off the fat before you reheat it.

SERVES 4

900g/2lb oxtail
2 tablespoons olive oil
50g/2oz rindless fat bacon,
    chopped
1 onion, chopped
1 garlic clove, finely chopped
225ml/8fl oz dry white wine
salt and freshly ground black
    pepper

about 300ml/½ pint hot beef
    stock
2 celery sticks, cut into
    4cm/1½in lengths
4 tomatoes, skinned and
    quartered
chopped parsley, to garnish

Cut the oxtail into 5cm/2in pieces, wash and dry well. Heat the oil in a flameproof casserole and sauté the bacon, onion and garlic until the onion is transparent. Add the oxtail and cook on all sides until brown.

Add the wine and season with a little salt and pepper. Cover and braise over a gentle heat for about 2 hours, shaking the pan occasionally and adding a little stock from time to time to keep the oxtail moist.

About 30 minutes before the end of the cooking time, add the celery, and about 10 minutes before the end of cooking, throw in the tomatoes, mixing well. Taste and adjust the seasoning before serving sprinkled with chopped parsley.

VEGETABLES, PULSES, CHEESE AND EGGS

WHITE BEAN GOULASH

I adore pulses of any kind. A soothing Indian dal, a warming green pea and ham soup. Or a plate of mushy peas; a slab of pease pudding; braised lentils; a salad of white haricot beans and tuna fish tossed in lemon juice and olive oil with chopped onions. Or boiled ham with parsley sauce and butter beans. Or a wonderful *soupe au pistou* enriched with dried red beans. Not to mention a serious chilli con carne (heavy on the chillies and beans, light on the meat).

This delightful dish of dried white beans is a simple country recipe, the ingredients of which any self-respecting farmhouse would have permanently in its larder. Paprika or dried chillies, the meaty bone from a mountain air-cured ham, garlands of garlic, a barrel of olive oil and, of course, a sack of dried beans. But it is that kind of dish. You don't cook it until you have eaten all the prosciutto (ham), which will have taken weeks of lunches. It is a dish to do with good housekeeping. It is the essence of resourcefulness, so necessary to good eating. It is also very tasty, nutritious, filling and economical. Ho. Ho. Try it.

SERVES 4–6

450g/1lb dried flageolet beans
  or cannellini beans, soaked
  overnight
1.8 litres/3 pints water
1 ham bone
1 carrot, finely chopped
1 large onion, finely chopped
2 garlic cloves, chopped
1 thyme sprig
1 bay leaf
1 parsley sprig

salt
3 tablespoons olive oil
1 teaspoon mild paprika
½ teaspoon hot paprika
2 tablespoons chopped flat-leaf
  parsley
2 tablespoons white wine
  vinegar
150ml/5fl oz soured cream, to
  garnish
snipped chives, to garnish

Rinse the soaked beans in plenty of fresh water, then put them into a very large saucepan with the cold water to cover. Bring up to boiling point and boil rapidly for 10 minutes. (It is a good idea to do this with all dried beans as some of them contain toxins that need to be destroyed.)

Put the ham bone into the saucepan with the beans and add the carrot, half the onion, 1 garlic clove, the thyme, bay leaf and parsley. Cover and simmer over a low heat for 1½–2 hours until the beans are really tender. Season with a little salt about halfway through cooking.

When the beans are cooked, remove the bone, bay leaf and thyme. Shred any meat from the bone that hasn't already fallen off and return it to the saucepan.

Heat the oil in a frying pan and gently fry the remaining onion and garlic for about 5 minutes. Add the mild and hot paprika and sauté for 2 more minutes. Stir into the saucepan with the parsley and vinegar and cook for 10 minutes. Season with salt and more paprika, if necessary. Ladle into bowls, spoon some soured cream on top and sprinkle with the chives.

FRIED RICE WITH BASIL AND PORK

I like this dish so much that when I go to stay with my friend Khun Akorn at his magnificent Tong Sai Bay Hotel in Koh Samui I have it for breakfast, I have it for lunch and I have it for supper. What is so enjoyable are the spicy and flavoursome slivers of pork among the chunks and strips of fresh raw pineapple, spring onions, cucumber and tomato. The crunchiness and sweetness of the vegetables contrasts exquisitely with the spiciness of the rest.

SERVES 4

3 tablespoons groundnut oil
175g/6oz loin of pork, diced or thinly sliced
3 tablespoons deseeded and finely chopped green chilli pepper
2 tablespoons finely chopped shallot
3 garlic cloves, finely chopped
¼ teaspoon freshly ground white pepper
about 4 cups steamed long-grain rice

2 tablespoons soft light brown sugar
1 tablespoon light soy sauce
90ml/3fl oz fish sauce
5 tablespoons roughly chopped fresh basil leaves
sliced cucumber, spring onions, fresh pineapple chunks, tomato – anything you like – to garnish

Heat the oil in a wok or large frying pan and add the pork, chilli pepper, shallot, garlic and pepper, and stir-fry for 3–4 minutes. Add the rice, sugar, soy sauce and fish sauce. Stir well and stir-fry for about 3 minutes, or until the rice is heated through. Add the basil leaves, garnish and serve.

RICE ON THE SIDE

The Spanish name for this dish, *Arroz a banda*, means rice on its own – abandoned rice. It is one of those dishes born out of the poverty of former times when perhaps the family income only supported the purchase of basic goods. The inventive house-keeper would maybe buy a fish head to make some soup or stock with which to flavour that constant staple, rice. For a special treat, some inexpensive pieces of squid would be thrown in, as an apology for the mountains of prawns and mussels that the booted and horsed classes would eat.

Like so many simple dishes born from necessity, it is quite delicious. It is virtually a fishless, meatless paella. The rich fish stock enriches and infuses the rice.

SERVES 4

FOR THE PICADA:
6 tablespoons olive oil
1 dried sweet red pepper, cored, deseeded and chopped
2 garlic cloves, chopped
a few strands of saffron
salt and freshly ground black pepper

225g/8oz fresh squidlets (small squid), cleaned and chopped
3 tablespoons Fresh Tomato Sauce (see page 159)
350g/12oz short-grain rice
1.2 litres/2 pints good fish stock – this is very important

To make the *picada*, heat the oil in a very large paella or frying pan. Cook the pepper and garlic together for 2–3 minutes, then transfer them to a blender, reserving the oil. Add the saffron with some salt and pepper and blend until smooth. Reserve until later.

Add the squidlets to the pan and fry them briefly, then stir in the fresh tomato sauce. Tip in the rice and add the fish stock. A really good fish stock is essential as the essence of this dish is that it tastes of the sea, without actually containing much seafood.

Add the red pepper *picada* to the pan and stir through, then cook gently for about 20–25 minutes, until the rice is cooked and tender and the liquid has been absorbed.

Serve this wondrously simple and satisfying dish with a bowl of garlic mayonnaise, a recipe for which you will find on page 161.

AFGHAN CURRY

I have named this dish after the famous train known as the Ghan that goes between Adelaide and Alice Springs. We were filming in a desperately remote location near the Ross River when suddenly we were attacked by a bus load of models who, incredibly, had chosen the same location to shoot a catalogue for the 'Spring Collection'. Naturally, we surrendered very quickly and decided to have a party. I only had a basic stock of vegetables with me that day so I concocted this sensational fruit and vegetable curry that the girls ate with relish because, the poor things, it was an unusually cold day in the middle of the Australian winter with a biting wind and they had to smile bravely, clad only in their bikinis and other light summer attire.

SERVES 4

1 teaspoon coriander seeds
1 teaspoon mustard seeds
1 teaspoon fennel seeds
2 garlic cloves, crushed
2.5cm/1in piece of fresh root
   ginger, chopped
2 medium green chilli peppers,
   deseeded and chopped
2 tablespoons red curry paste
1 tablespoon sesame oil
2 tablespoons vegetable oil
1 onion, sliced

2 carrots, sliced lengthways
100g/4oz cauliflower florets
2 small leeks, sliced
1 eating apple, cored and sliced
1 pear, cored and sliced
75g/3oz dwarf green beans
50g/2oz dried apricots
575ml/1 pint coconut milk
2 tablespoons fish sauce
juice of 2 limes
chopped coriander leaves,
   to garnish

Using a mortar and pestle, crunch the coriander, mustard and fennel seeds. Mix with the garlic, ginger, chillies and red curry paste.

Heat the sesame and vegetable oils in a very large pan and fry the spice mixture for 2 minutes, stirring constantly. Pop in the onion and fry for 2 further minutes, then add all the remaining ingredients. Bring to the boil, then reduce the heat and simmer gently, covered, for about 20 minutes, until cooked. Garnish with the coriander and serve with mounds of plain boiled rice.

SPINACH WITH RAISINS
AND PINE NUTS

It is harder work being the cameraman on a Floyd shoot than it is being the presenter. My cameraman, the legendary, world-famous Clive North, works extremely hard, and the camera is quite heavy as well.

So it is important that he has three square meals a day. A carefully balanced breakfast comprising fruit juice, cereal and yoghurt, a sensible-sized portion of rashers, eggs, mushrooms and tomatoes, some fresh brown toast and coffee. At lunchtime he prefers to tuck into something substantial yet simple; maybe a couple of T-bone steaks or half-a-dozen lamb chops. But for dinner he likes to prowl round the back streets of whatever city we happen to be in, looking for an interesting restaurant.

And in Barcelona Clive found a little place just around the corner from the Havana Palace Hotel and came back raving about a dish he had had as a starter – Spinach with Raisins and Pine Nuts. In fact, he was not only raving about it, he became absolutely hooked on it and, for the remainder of the shoot, he demanded this easy but tasty dish everywhere he went. So I dedicate this snack to Clive.

SERVES 4 AS A STARTER OR SIDE DISH

50g/2oz seedless raisins or
   sultanas
900g/2lb fresh spinach,
   thoroughly washed and
   trimmed, or Swiss chard
   or kale

3 tablespoons olive oil
1 small garlic clove, crushed
3 tablespoons pine nuts
salt and freshly ground black
   pepper
croûtons, to garnish

Pour some boiling water over the raisins or sultanas, and leave them to plump up while you cook the spinach. Do this by packing it into a large saucepan, adding just a little boiling water and a sprinkling of salt. If you have young, tender leaves, just blanch them for a couple of moments. If you have older spinach, cook it for longer, maybe 10 minutes or so, and chop or shred it so it is more of a mushy mess. The first method is the Chinese way, the second is the Indian. It does depend on whether you have young, succulent spinach leaves. Drain well in a colander, squeezing out the liquid by pressing the spinach down with the back of a spoon. Now chop it roughly.

Heat the oil in a frying pan and sauté the garlic gently for a couple of minutes. Add the spinach, pine nuts and drained, soaked raisins or sultanas. Season with a little more salt if needed, and some pepper. Cook gently for about 5 more minutes, then serve with croûtons sprinkled over.

FRESH BROAD BEANS AND BACON

Until you try this little snack from the Garden of Eden itself, you will have no idea how truly wonderful it is. I first cooked it forty years ago during one of my midnight raids on my grandmother's larder, where I found a bowl of leftover cooked broad beans and some rashers of streaky bacon. What inspired me to do it I will never know but I just chopped up the bacon and on a whim tipped in the broad beans. My grandmother, who disapproved of my raiding her larder, was so impressed that she didn't scold me!

SERVES 4

900g/2lb fresh broad beans from your garden – which you were tending when the guests unexpectedly arrived
a dash of olive oil
1–2 garlic cloves, chopped or left whole, as you like
at least 225g/8oz back bacon, diced

freshly ground black pepper
freshly grated Parmesan, Pecorino or Cheddar cheese, whatever takes your fancy – slivers of fresh goat's cheese would be good too – to serve

Shell the beans and blanch them for 3 minutes in boiling salted water, then drain.

Heat your largest frying pan and add the oil, garlic, bacon

and the drained beans. Mill over lots of pepper and fry gently until the bacon is cooked and the beans are tender. Serve with the cheese handed separately in a bowl.

PS Broad beans don't come from freezer chests.

ONION TART

Walk along any street in France and you will pass superb shops selling fabulous breads, cakes, pies and tarts. Well, don't – it's really stupid to pass one of these superb shops without entering, especially early in the morning when everything is so aromatically exciting, still warm and very fresh. Buy a slice of tart. The recipe that I have included here is from Alsace. Down in the south of France they have another version. It is essentially the same but garnished with a slice of hard-boiled egg, a slice of tomato, a couple of anchovies and a stoned olive – they call it *Pissaladière*. Both are brilliant – and so am I!

SERVES 6–8

FOR THE PASTRY:
300g/10oz plain flour
150g/5oz butter, cut in small
   pieces
a pinch of salt
1 egg, beaten

FOR THE FILLING:
300g/10oz fromage blanc
salt and freshly ground black
   pepper
2 pinches of freshly grated
   nutmeg
90g/3½oz lean smoked bacon,
   finely diced
300g/10oz onions, finely
   chopped
butter for frying
4 eggs, separated

First make the pastry. Sift the flour into a bowl, make a well in the middle and add the butter, salt and egg. Mix with your fingertips until the mixture forms a ball. Knead on a floured board until the dough is completely smooth. Roll into a ball, cover with a floured tea-towel and allow to rest at room temperature for a couple of hours.

Then roll out the pastry and use it to line a well-buttered quiche or flan dish. Prick the bottom all over with a fork and bake blind for 20 minutes in the oven preheated to 190°C/375°F/gas mark 5.

Mix the fromage blanc with a little salt, pepper and nutmeg. (Remember that the smoked bacon is already quite salty.) Beat until smooth.

Fry the bacon and onions in butter until the onions are transparent. Drain off the butter. Add the bacon and onions to the fromage blanc.

Beat in the egg yolks. Whisk the egg whites until stiff, then fold into the mixture. Pour into the baked pastry shell and bake in the oven preheated to 220°C/425°F/gas mark 7 for 30–45 minutes until the tart is chestnut-brown all over. Turn out of the dish and serve hot.

CLASSIC PIPÉRADE

Although it is many years since we filmed *Floyd on France*, people still gleefully mock me about this dish. I was cooking it for an imperious French lady who, observing my culinary skills with dismay, horror and incredulity, told me very clearly that I did not know what I was doing. In fact, the recipe *does* work, *is* good, and Madame still sends me a Christmas card each year.

SERVES 4

oil and butter for frying

2 red peppers, cored, deseeded and chopped

1 green pepper, cored, deseeded and chopped

4 ripe tomatoes, skinned, deseeded and chopped

1 garlic clove, finely chopped

½ red chilli pepper or *piment d'espellete* (see opposite) or a pinch of ground paprika

chopped thyme

chopped parsley

1 bay leaf

salt and freshly ground black pepper

1 teaspoon caster sugar (the secret ingredient given to me by Mimi in Biarritz)

6 eggs

4 slices of Bayonne ham or any cured ham (Parma, for example) or good bacon

Heat some oil and butter together in a frying pan and cook the peppers, tomatoes and garlic, together with all the spices and seasonings (including the sugar), until very soft. Beat the eggs with a little cold water and stir them in until set but creamy, as for scrambled eggs. Fish out the bay leaf.

Meanwhile, fry the ham or bacon and serve with the pipérade mixture.

PS Espellete, a small town in the Basque Country, is the centre of France's red pepper powder industry. The locals and the cognoscenti wouldn't dream of using any other type.

POTATO OMELETTE

Fourteen-year-old beach bar cooks can make *tortillas* to perfection. All grannies – Spanish ones, that is – can make them to perfection. And yet, seemingly the simplest of dishes, it is one of the most difficult in which to achieve perfection. Do not make the mistake of thinking it is just fried potatoes with egg over the top.

The secret lies in having a heavy, well-used iron frying pan and in using the finest-quality olive oil and chunks of extremely waxy potatoes. And then in cooking those potatoes in a generous amount of the oil for a long time, so that they have absorbed the flavour of the oil and are neither falling apart nor raw hard cubes. The potatoes are almost boiled rather than fried in the oil.

Most important of all, when the *tortilla* is cooked, it must be eaten – after it has been allowed to sit for half an hour or so – like a slice of cake. It is also delicious served cold later in the day as a *tapa*. Remember, these kinds of omelette were made for people to take to work for their mid-morning break or their lunch in the fields or factories. Show me a good Spanish omelette-maker and I will show you a sensitive cook. It is not a dish to play or joke with.

SERVES 4

225ml/8fl oz olive oil salt
4 large potatoes, cut into chunks 4 large eggs, beaten
1 medium onion, thinly sliced

Heat the oil in a frying pan – do use olive oil, otherwise your *tortilla* will be a poor relation to anything the Spaniards cook. Add the potatoes, a handful at a time, and then the onion. Stir well and season with a good sprinkling of salt.

Cook gently for about 20 minutes or so. The general idea is to stew the potatoes in the oil, rather than to get them brown and crisp. Stir them from time to time and if you find they have 'caked', just break them up gently. When they are cooked, remove the potatoes from the pan. Pour out the oil and reserve it. Mix the potatoes with the beaten eggs and season with a bit more salt.

Wipe out the frying pan with some kitchen paper, then reheat 2 tablespoons of the reserved oil, until it is really hot. Tip in the potato mixture. Lower the heat and shake the pan frequently to prevent sticking. Cook gently until the potatoes begin to brown underneath and the mixture is set. Next, find a plate the same size as the frying pan and pop it over the pan. Flip the whole lot over – you should now have your *tortilla* on the plate, with the cooked side uppermost.

Add 1 more tablespoon of oil to the pan and slide the omelette back in (do this with confidence, it is always the best way). Cook the *tortilla* for another 4–5 minutes, or until it is brown on the second side.

Serve in wedges. Simple, but truly wonderful! Try it at luke-warm temperature, as the Spanish do, or cold with pickles and chutney.

MIGAS

Serves 4

400g/14oz stale bread, crusts removed and cut into cubes
2 tablespoons cold water
3 tablespoons olive oil
100g/4oz bacon, chopped
3 garlic cloves, chopped
1 teaspoon paprika
¼ teaspoon ground cumin

salt and freshly ground black pepper
1 small onion, finely chopped
50g/2oz serrano or prosciutto ham, chopped
4 eggs, for frying (more if you're hungry)

Put the cubes of bread into a bowl and sprinkle the water over the top, stirring well. Cover and set aside.

Heat 2 tablespoons of the oil in a large, heavy-based frying pan. Add the bacon and cook until it is fairly crisp. Lift out with a slotted spoon and set this aside too. Now add 1 chopped garlic clove to the pan and cook until brown. Fish it out and discard.

Go back to the bread and season it with the paprika and cumin, then some salt and pepper. Mix it well, then add to the frying pan over a very low heat. Cook it very slowly for about 20 minutes, stirring occasionally, without browning.

Meanwhile, heat the remaining tablespoon of oil in a separate pan and sauté the onion for a few minutes until soft. Add the remaining garlic and cook for a couple of minutes longer. Pop in the serrano ham and the bacon you cooked earlier, stir everything together and cook for 2 minutes to heat through.

When the bread is done, tip the onion mixture into it, stirring well. Quickly fry some eggs and serve with this mixture.

LENTIL SALAD

SERVES 4

225g/8oz brown, green or
yellow lentils, soaked and
rinsed
1 small onion, peeled and
halved
1 carrot, peeled and halved
1 garlic clove, peeled
2 whole cloves
1 bay leaf
salt
3 tablespoons chopped parsley,
to garnish

FOR THE DRESSING:
4 tablespoons olive oil
1 tablespoon red wine vinegar
2 tablespoons minced onion
1 garlic clove, crushed
2 tablespoons chopped sweet
red pepper or pimiento
freshly ground black pepper
salt

Put the lentils, onion, carrot, garlic, cloves and bay leaf into a
large pot and cover with some salted water. Bring to the boil,
then reduce the heat, cover and simmer gently for about 30
minutes, until the lentils are just tender. Drain in a colander and
rinse. Throw out everything except the lentils and carrot. Chop
the carrot into dice, mix with the lentils and transfer to a serving bowl.

Mix together all the ingredients for the dressing and pour
over the lentils, stirring through gently with a wooden spoon.
Allow the salad to stand for an hour or two, so that the lentils
absorb the flavour of the dressing. Just before serving, sprinkle
over the parsley.

COUNTRY TERRINE

The simple French country terrine, if made at home with fresh ingredients and served chilled with a few gherkins, some olives and some sweet summer tomatoes, is one of the finest hors d'œuvres there is. Recipes vary from area to area, but they are all roughly based on pork, veal and pig's liver, and they tend to be quite fatty and crumbly, which is nice. Here is a typical version.

SERVES 4–8

450g/1lb belly of pork, finely chopped *not* minced
225g/8oz pig's liver, minced
350g/12oz veal, minced
2 garlic cloves, crushed
6 black peppercorns, crushed
4 juniper berries, crushed
a pinch of ground mace
salt and freshly ground black pepper

1 large wine-glass of dry white wine
a generous splash of brandy
100g/4oz sheet of pork fat or slice of speck (cured pork fat), half cut into little cubes and half cut into strips 1cm/½in thick

Mix together all the ingredients except the strips of fat and leave to stand for a couple of hours in a cool place.

Tip the lot into a terrine and lay the strips of fat over the top. Put the terrine into a bain-marie and cook in the oven preheated to 170°C/325°F/gas mark 3 for about 1½ hours. Allow to cool for 24 hours before serving.

FLOYD'S FONDUE

A world without cheese and wine is not worth living in. A wedge of Stilton and a glass of port, a slice of Cheddar and a pickled onion, a pyramid of goat and a glass of Rhône, they are of this world, but in reality come from heaven. Without cheese life isn't worth living. When I am satiated by meat and fine food, but am hungry for something tasty and light, a fondue springs to mind. Easy to prepare, fun to do; I offer you this typical fondue recipe.

SERVES 4

1 garlic clove
290g/10½oz Emmenthal cheese
250g/9oz Gruyère cheese
300ml/½ pint dry white wine
1 tablespoon lemon juice
25ml/1fl oz Kirsch
3 teaspoons cornflour

2 tablespoons finely chopped
   herbs such as parsley, chives
   and chervil
freshly ground black pepper
cubes of bread for dipping in
   the fondue

Cut the garlic clove and rub it around the fondue dish. Cut the cheese into small dice that will melt evenly and put into the dish with the wine and lemon juice. Bubble it up gently, whisking constantly, until the mixture is smooth, then add the Kirsch mixed with the cornflour. Stir in herbs and season to taste. Serve with cubes of bread to dip into the fondue.

PUDDINGS AND BREAD

PEARS IN CHIANTI

Robust red wine, such as Chianti, goes beautifully with pears.

SERVES 6

175g/6oz caster sugar
725ml/1¼ pints red wine
a few strips of orange zest

1 cinnamon stick
6 firm pears with the stalks on
Mascarpone cheese, to serve

Dissolve the sugar in the wine in a large, heavy-based saucepan, and add the orange zest and cinnamon stick.

Peel the pears, leaving the stalks on, and cut a small slice from the base of each so that it stands upright.

Place the pears in the red wine mixture, pour in boiling water to come to the tops of the fruit, cover and cook over a gentle heat for about 15–20 minutes until tender.

Remove from the heat and leave the pears to cool in the wine for several hours, turning them occasionally to ensure an even crimson colour.

Carefully transfer the pears to a serving dish. Remove the orange zest and cinnamon stick from the wine mixture and boil for 5–10 minutes, until reduced to a syrupy consistency. Pour over the pears and leave to cool, then chill for 1 hour. Serve with creamy Mascarpone cheese.

PEAR TART

This is the most wonderful pear dessert using ratafias or little Italian Amarettis and pear liqueur to enhance the delicate flavour of the fruit. It should really be served warm with whipped cream to tickle the taste-buds.

SERVES 6

FOR THE PASTRY CASE:
100g/4oz butter, softened
2 tablespoons cold water
25g/1oz icing sugar
225g/8oz plain flour

FOR THE FRUIT:
3 even-sized Comice pears
75g/3oz sugar
150ml/5fl oz water

FOR THE FILLING:
50g/2oz ratafia biscuits or little
   Italian Amarettis, available
   from good delicatessens
2 tablespoons pear liqueur
175ml/6fl oz double cream
2 large eggs
icing sugar

First make the pastry: make sure that the butter is soft enough to work with, but do not melt it – room temperature is ideal. Put the butter, water, sugar and one-third of the flour into a large bowl. Mix well, using a wooden spoon, to make a tacky paste. Gradually work in the remaining flour, then knead until smooth. Roll the pastry out thinly on a lightly floured surface and use a little over half of this to line a deep 20cm/8in flan ring. Don't roll the pastry too thickly or it will not cook evenly or become crisp.

Bake blind in the oven preheated to 190°C/375°F/gas mark 5 for about 20 minutes, or until lightly browned and firm. Allow to cool. The remainder of the pastry can be used to make some fruit tartlets or a smaller fruit flan.

Thinly peel, halve and core the pears. Put the sugar and water into a pan, add the pears and poach for about 10 minutes until just tender.

Sprinkle the ratafias or Amarettis with the pear liqueur. Whisk together the cream and eggs and stir into the biscuits. Drain the pears and arrange neatly over the base of the flan case, cut-side down. Spoon over the filling. Bake in the centre of the oven preheated to 190°C/375°F/gas mark 5 for 45 minutes, until firm and set. Sprinkle with icing sugar and return to the oven for a few minutes to brown lightly.

PRUNE TART

Serves 4–6

For the pastry case:
450g/1lb plain flour
2 eggs, beaten
a pinch of salt
a wine-glass of double cream
225g/8oz butter, softened and
    cut into pieces

For the filling:
900g/2lb stoned prunes,
    cooked with sugar
3 tablespoons sugar

Sift the flour into a large bowl. Make a well in the centre and add the eggs, salt and enough cream to make a dough. Add the butter bit by bit. Mix well, roll up and leave in the refrigerator for about 2 hours.

Roll out the pastry on a floured board and line a pie dish with about two-thirds of it. Squash some of the prunes together and put them into the pie shell. Arrange the remaining prunes on top. Cut the remaining pastry into 1cm/½in strips and criss-cross the tart with them in a lattice pattern.

Bake in the oven preheated to 200°C/400°F/gas mark 6 for 35–40 minutes and, when nearly done, dust the tart with the sugar, then return to the oven to brown.

Serve hot or cold.

ZABAGLIONE

Whisk Marsala with egg yolks and sugar for a frothy dessert or, indeed, a pick-me-up for those under the weather – Zabaglione!

This is simple to make but quite hard work. Your whisking hand needs to be in good shape.

SERVES 4

4 large free-range egg yolks
8 tablespoons caster sugar
Marsala

Whisk together the egg yolks and sugar in a bowl. Place the bowl over a pan of gently simmering water. Pour in the Marsala and whisk like hell until you have a smooth, frothy, thick custard-like mixture. Serve immediately in glasses with sweet biscuits.

SANTIAGO CAKE

I am absolutely hopeless at cooking puddings, but I do love eating them. In Spain the ubiquitous *Tarta de Santiago* – a beautiful almond-flavoured cake that is eaten as a pudding – is absolutely scrumptious when freshly baked.

MAKES 12 SLICES

3 large eggs	225g/8oz ground almonds
225g/8oz caster sugar	grated zest of ½ lemon
100g/4oz butter	sifted icing sugar and a few
175g/6oz self-raising flour	chopped almonds, to
125ml/4fl oz water	decorate

Break the eggs into a food processor, add the sugar, butter, flour and water and whizz together for a minute or so until all the ingredients are well blended. (If you don't have a processor, then I'm afraid you'll have to work quite hard for about 15 minutes beating the ingredients together properly by hand.) Tip in the ground almonds and lemon zest and whizz for a few seconds, or beat by hand, just to mix. (You don't put the almonds in at the beginning because they would become overworked and oily.)

When everything is well blended, tip the mixture into a lined, well-greased, 20cm/8in cake tin. Level the surface and bake in the oven preheated to 180°C/350°F/gas mark 4 for about 1 hour or until a skewer inserted into the centre of the cake comes out clean.

Remove the cake from the oven and allow to cool in the tin for 10 minutes, then turn it out on to a wire rack and leave to cool completely. Dust with icing sugar and sprinkle some chopped almonds over the top.

KEY LIME PIE

Ideally this should be made with Key limes from the Florida Keys or the Caribbean, which have a wonderful strong tart flavour.

SERVES 6–8

FOR THE CRUST:
100g/4oz butter, softened
175g/6oz Graham crackers or
    digestive biscuits, crumbled
¼ teaspoon vanilla extract

FOR THE FILLING:
6 egg yolks
1 x 400g/14oz can of sweetened
    condensed milk
175ml/6fl oz fresh lime juice
2 teaspoons grated lime zest

FOR THE MERINGUE:
6 egg whites
1 teaspoon vanilla extract
1 teaspoon cream of tartar
¼ teaspoon salt
225g/8oz caster sugar

Make the crust by blending the softened butter with the cracker or digestive biscuit crumbs and vanilla extract. Spread and press the mixture around the bottom and sides of a 23cm/9in pie dish. Make the filling by blending the egg yolks with the condensed milk. Add the lime juice. Pour the filling into the pie shell. Bake in the oven preheated to 180°C/350°F/gas mark 4 for 15 minutes.

Meanwhile, to make the meringue, beat the egg whites until frothy. Add the vanilla extract, cream of tartar and salt and beat slightly. Add the sugar gradually, beating well. Continue beating until the mixture forms stiff peaks. Swirl over the pie filling and bake in the oven preheated to 200°C/400°F/gas mark 6 for about 7–10 minutes or until the meringue is browned. Allow to cool and refrigerate before serving.

BAKED APPLE DUMPLINGS

I can remember walking into the kitchen after school and the sweet aroma of these dumplings cooking stirring my taste-buds.

SERVES 4

450g/1lb shortcrust pastry
4 even-sized cooking apples,
  peeled and cored
50g/2oz soft light brown sugar

milk, to glaze
caster sugar
clotted cream or custard
  (see page 154), to serve

Divide the pastry into 4 equal pieces and roll each into a 20–25cm/8–10in round.

Place one apple on each pastry round and fill the centres of the apples with brown sugar. Moisten the edges of the pastry with water and gather the edges to the top, pressing well, to seal them together. Turn the dumplings over. Brush the tops with milk and sprinkle with caster sugar. Decorate with pastry leaves if desired.

Place on a greased tray and bake towards the top of the oven preheated to 220°C/425°F/gas mark 7 for 10 minutes, then reduce the temperature to 160°C/325°F/gas mark 3 and continue to bake for a further 30 minutes until the apples are soft.

Serve hot or cold with clotted cream or home-made English custard.

MARMALADE AND SPICE SUET PUDDING

Bring back the steamed pudding! I will! So here is one of my family's favourite suet puds.

SERVES 6

100g/4oz self-raising flour
a pinch of salt
1 teaspoon ground mixed spice
100g/4oz shredded suet
100g/4oz fresh white
  breadcrumbs

25g/1oz soft light brown sugar
175g/6oz orange or grapefruit
  marmalade
milk, water or orange juice
  to mix
custard (see page 154), to serve

Sift the flour, salt and spice into a bowl. Add the suet, breadcrumbs and sugar and mix well. Stir in the marmalade and a little milk, water or orange juice to make a stiff but manageable dough.

Tip into a well-greased 1.2 litre/2 pint pudding basin – the mixture should two-thirds fill the basin. Cover the top of the pudding with a double layer of pleated greaseproof paper and secure with string. Steam for 2½ hours (top up the water level in the pan with boiling water as necessary).

PS Don't forget the custard and extra whisky marmalade on top.

ALSATIAN CHEESE CAKE

SERVES 4–6

FOR THE PASTRY CASE:
300g/10oz plain flour
150g/5oz butter, diced
7–15g/¼–½oz salt
1 tablespoon caster sugar
1 egg, beaten

FOR THE FILLING:
400g/14oz fromage blanc
90g/3½oz caster sugar
5 eggs, separated
50g/2oz flour, sifted
juice of 1 small lemon
1 teaspoon vanilla extract

First make the pastry case. Sift the flour into a large bowl and make a well in the centre. Add the butter, salt, sugar and egg. Mix with your fingertips until well amalgamated and roll into a ball. Knead on a floured board until smooth. Wrap in a floured cloth and refrigerate for a couple of hours.

Roll out the pastry on a floured board to a thickness of about 5mm/¼in. Use to line a well-buttered 20cm/8in flan tin with a removable base. Prick all over with a fork and bake blind in the oven preheated to 190°C/375°F/gas mark 5 for 20 minutes.

Beat together the fromage blanc, sugar, egg yolks, flour, lemon juice and vanilla. Whisk the egg whites until stiff and fold into the mixture. Pour into the baked pastry case and bake in the oven preheated to 220°C/425°F/gas mark 7 for 30 minutes until a rich brown all over. Slide out on to a cooling rack and leave upside down until cool. This will keep the surface smooth. Serve right side up.

REAL CUSTARD SAUCE

SERVES 4–6

2 free-range egg yolks	1 vanilla pod
1 tablespoon sugar	300ml/½ pint milk

Beat the egg yolks lightly in a bowl. Heat the sugar with the vanilla pod and milk in a pan until hot but not boiling. Remove the vanilla pod and whisk the mixture into the egg yolks. Place the bowl over a pan of hot water or place the mixture in the top of a double boiler and cook, stirring constantly, for about 20–25 minutes, until the custard thickens slightly and will coat the back of a spoon.

Serve warm or cold.

CHOCOLATE FUDGE PUDDING

SERVES 4–6

175g/6oz self-raising flour
135g/4½oz caster sugar
100g/4oz cocoa powder
50g/2oz butter, melted
125ml/4fl oz milk
 2 tablespoons brandy

175g/6oz walnuts, chopped
175g/6oz soft light brown
  sugar
400ml/14fl oz hot water
 whipped cream, to serve

Mix together the flour, caster sugar and half the cocoa. Pour the melted butter into the milk mixed with the brandy, then blend with the dry ingredients. Stir in the walnuts. Spoon the mixture into a greased and lined 22.5cm/9in square tin. Mix the remaining cocoa with the brown sugar and sprinkle over the top. Pour over the hot water and bake in the oven pre-heated to 190°C/375°F/gas mark 5 for 35 minutes.

While still hot, cut into squares, invert each on to a serving dish and spoon over the sauce left in the tin. Serve with plenty of whipped cream.

BREAD PUDDING WITH WHISKEY SAUCE

SERVES 16–20

300g/10oz breadcrumbs made
 from stale French bread
900ml/1½ pints milk
400g/14oz sugar
8 tablespoons melted butter
3 eggs
2 teaspoons vanilla extract
165g/5½oz raisins
90g/3½oz desiccated coconut
100g/4oz pecan nuts, chopped

1 teaspoon ground cinnamon
1 teaspoon freshly grated
 nutmeg

FOR THE SAUCE:
100g/4oz butter
315g/10½oz caster sugar
2 egg yolks
about 100ml/4fl oz bourbon or
 other American whiskey

Combine all the pudding ingredients in a large bowl: the mixture should be moist but not soupy. Transfer to a 23 x 30cm/ 9 x 12in buttered baking dish and bake in the oven preheated to 180°C/350°F/gas mark 4 for about 1¼ hours or until the top is golden-brown.

To make the sauce, cream the butter and sugar together in a pan over medium heat until all the butter is absorbed. Remove from the heat and blend in the egg yolks. Gradually add the bourbon to taste, stirring constantly. Allow the sauce to cool a little before serving – it will thicken as it does so. Serve warm over the warm pudding.

CHURROS

I love 'street food'. It's fun munching as you wander through crowded streets watching the world go by and in Spain *churros* are delightful little confections of light batter, deep-fried, sometimes dredged in sugar and sometimes eaten with salt as a savoury niblet. They are like a very, very light doughnut, only they are not, and are similar to the *beignets* you find in France. They are popular at breakfast time, dipped into coffee or chocolate, and they are also found on street stalls at *fiestas*.

SERVES 4

225ml/8fl oz water
5 tablespoons oil
½ teaspoon salt
200g/7oz plain flour

vegetable oil for frying
icing or caster sugar
½ teaspoon grated lemon zest
½ teaspoon ground cinnamon

Put the water, oil and salt into a small saucepan and bring up to the boil. Meanwhile, measure out the flour. As soon as the water is boiling, shoot the flour into the pan, all at once, beating it in with a wooden spoon to make a smooth, stiff ball of paste.

Let the paste cool down a little, then put it into a large piping bag, fitted with a star nozzle. Pipe out strips about 10cm/4in long, or make loop shapes instead. Heat the oil – it must be a minimum of 2cm/¾in deep – and fry about 4 at a time, bearing in mind that they swell as they cook. When golden-brown, remove with a slotted spoon and drain on kitchen paper.

Dust the *churros* while they are still hot in the icing or caster sugar mixed with the lemon zest and cinnamon and eat at once.

IRISH BROWN SODA BREAD

There must be dozens of different versions of soda bread but the one that I use was given to me by Myrtle Allen (see her Irish Stew recipe on page 106). A thickly buttered slice of this bread, topped with thick slices of Irish smoked salmon, finely sliced onion, capers and a dollop of soured cream is a delight.

Buttermilk or whey are excellent substitutes for sour milk in this recipe.

MAKES 1 × 675G/1½LB LOAF

450g/1lb wholemeal flour
150g/5oz strong white flour
50g/2oz oatmeal
1 teaspoon bicarbonate of soda

1 teaspoon salt
450–700ml/16–24fl oz sour
   milk, or fresh milk soured
   with juice of ½ lemon

Mix the ingredients very thoroughly. Moisten with the sour milk to form a soft dough. Knead lightly. Form into a round, mark with a cross and bake in the oven preheated to 220°C/425°F/gas mark 7 for 30–45 minutes.

ꞂAUCES AND STOCKS

FRESH TOMATO SAUCE

Fresh tomato sauce is one of the most useful and versatile sauces of all. Simple pasta with this rich red concoction is delightful. A pork chop grilled on the barbecue will smile when the sauce is poured over it. You can subtly alter the sauce's flavour, for example, by adding masses of chopped fresh basil, or fresh mint, or chillies – the possibilities are endless. Spanish and Italian cooks of the old school often cook the sauce by poaching it in sealed kilner jars. Take advantage of the season when tomatoes are in glut to line the shelves of your larder for later.

Make about 300ml/½ pint

4 tablespoons extra virgin
  olive oil
1 onion, finely chopped
1 large garlic clove, crushed
1kg/2¼lb very ripe plum
  tomatoes, skinned, deseeded
  and chopped

1 tablespoon chopped basil
1 teaspoon caster sugar
a little wine vinegar
salt and freshly ground black
  pepper

Heat the oil in a large, heavy-based saucepan. Add the onion and fry for about 3–4 minutes, then add the garlic, tomatoes, basil, sugar, a few drops of wine vinegar and salt and pepper. Simmer slowly until you get a rich, thick sauce.

MY MUM'S PARSLEY SAUCE

I have eaten at the highest and the lowest tables around the world. I have paid exorbitant bills in fine restaurants, I have eaten bread and lard sprinkled with paprika in a desolate café in Budapest. I know many fine chefs and cooks but one of the best happens to be my mother and her parsley sauce is excellent.

SERVES 4

50g/2oz butter
3 tablespoons plain flour
300ml/½ pint warm fish stock
300ml/½ pint warm milk
salt and freshly ground black
    pepper

6 tablespoons very finely
    chopped parsley
1 egg yolk
1 tablespoon double cream

Melt the butter in a pan. Stir in the flour and cook for about 3 minutes, being careful not to let it burn. Add the stock, stirring constantly, then add the milk and season with salt and pepper. Simmer until a smooth sauce has been achieved. Add the parsley and simmer for 5 more minutes. And just before you serve it, whisk in the egg yolk and cream rapidly.

• Obviously you can flavour this sauce as you wish – with, say, capers or mushrooms instead of the parsley.

• For a *sauce normande*, reduce the sauce (without the parsley) by about a quarter and add 10 cooked mussels, a few fresh prawns and a couple of langoustines.

• Or you can substitute chicken or ham bouillon for the fish stock to make different-tasting sauces.

AÏOLI

This magnificent garlic mayonnaise is to a plate of food (whether it be sauce for prawns, a piece of poached salt cod, a fish soup or simply a plate of boiled new potatoes) what the Provençal sun is to the vineyards of the Côtes-du-Rhône – it is indispensable.

SERVES 4

8 garlic cloves
2 free-range egg yolks
450ml/¾ pint good olive oil

juice of 1 lemon
salt and freshly ground white pepper

You should really crush the garlic in a pestle and mortar; then, with a whisk, stir in the egg yolks. Then you stir away madly, while you dribble in the olive oil until you have a thick, yellow mayonnaise. Last, you stir in the lemon juice and salt and pepper to taste.

Or you can put all the ingredients, except the olive oil, into a food processor, turn it on and pour in the oil, slowly but evenly, while the eggs and garlic are whizzing around. It will not be as good, but much quicker.

BARBECUE SAUCE

SERVES 4

2 garlic cloves
½ teaspoon salt
½ teaspoon paprika
4 tablespoons runny honey
3 tablespoons tomato purée

4 tablespoons orange juice
4 tablespoons white or red
  wine vinegar
6 tablespoons soy sauce

Crush the garlic and salt in a pestle and mortar. Then grind in
the paprika, stir in the honey followed by all the other ingredients, one at a time, stirring all the while. Or you could whizz it
in a food processor. Simmer the sauce for 5–10 minutes and
serve hot or cold.

THAI SOUP STOCK

MAKES 1.5 LITRES/2½–3½ PINTS

2.4 litres/4 pints water
675g/1½lb chicken, beef, pork
   or fish bones, depending on
   the flavour of the stock you
   need
2 celery sticks, chopped
2 onions, chopped

2 fresh coriander roots,
   chopped
4 Kaffir lime leaves
2.5cm/1in piece of fresh root
   ginger, chopped
salt and freshly ground black
   pepper

Put all the ingredients into a very large pan. Bring to the boil, then cover and simmer for about 1 hour, skimming the fat from time to time.

Strain through a fine sieve and discard all but the stock, then strain again, lining the sieve with muslin to achieve a clear liquid. Cool and refrigerate, then skim off any fat from the surface. Use within 2 days, or freeze and keep for up to 3 months. Use in soup recipes.

FISH STOCK

MAKES ABOUT 900ML/1½ PINTS

450g/1lb fish trimmings – heads, tails, leftover bones, etc.
1 onion, chopped
1 carrot, chopped
1 leek, chopped

a few white peppercorns
bouquet garni
150ml/5fl oz dry white wine
1 litre/1¾ pints water

Put all the ingredients into a large pan, bring to the boil, then reduce the heat. Cover and simmer very gently for 30 minutes. Cool slightly, then strain through a fine sieve. Cool completely, refrigerate and use within 1 day, or freeze and keep for up to 1 month.

CHICKEN STOCK

Makes about 900ml/1½ pints

1 chicken carcass and bones
  from a carved chicken
1 small carrot, chopped
1 onion, roughly chopped

1 turnip, roughly chopped
bouquet garni
1 litre/1¾ pints cold water

Put the chicken carcass into a large pan with the vegetables and bouquet garni. Cover with the water and bring to the boil, then reduce the heat, cover and simmer gently for a least 2 hours. Cool slightly, then strain through a very fine sieve. Cool completely, refrigerate and use within 2 days, or freeze and keep for up to 3 months.

GAME STOCK

If the stock is required for making a light sauce, use white wine instead of red.

MAKES ABOUT 1.6 LITRES/2¾ PINTS

oil

chopped leftover meat of any game such as duck, pigeon, pheasant, etc., including chopped carcasses, necks and giblets

1 onion, chopped

1 carrot, chopped

600ml/1 pint good red wine

600ml/1 pint veal stock

1 litre/1¾ pints water

some juniper berries, crushed

bouquet garni

Heat a little oil in a pan and brown the leftover game pieces. Add the onion and carrot and cook until they are softened but not browned. Add the wine, veal stock, water, juniper berries and bouquet garni and simmer for at least 2 hours, frequently skimming off any scum from the surface. Strain the stock through a very fine sieve, without forcing. Cool completely and refrigerate. Use within 2 days, or freeze and keep for up to 3 months.

BEEF STOCK

Makes about 1.5 litres/2½ pints

450g/1lb marrow bones
450g/1lb shin of beef, cut into
    chunks
2 litres/3½ pints cold water
1 carrot, sliced

1 onion, chopped
2 sticks of celery, sliced
½ teaspoon salt
bouquet garni

Brown the bones and the shin of beef in a roasting tin in a preheated oven, 200°C/400°F/gas mark 6, for about 30 minutes. Transfer to a large pan and cover with the water. Add the vegetables to the roasting pan and roast them for about 10 minutes, until browned. Tip them into the pan with the bones, add the salt and bouquet garni, then bring to the boil. Reduce the heat, cover and simmer for about 3–4 hours, skimming off any fat or scum from the surface from time to time.

Cool slightly, then strain through a fine sieve. Cool completely and refrigerate. Use within 2 days, or freeze and use within 3 months.

VEGETABLE STOCK

MAKES ABOUT 1.2 LITRES/2 PINTS

1 large onion, stuck with
  whole cloves
2 carrots, sliced
2 leeks, chopped
bouquet garni
wedge of lemon

750ml/1¼ pints cold water
750ml/1¼ pints dry white wine
  or dry cider
1 tablespoon white wine
  vinegar

Put all the ingredients into a large pan. Bring to the boil, then reduce the heat, cover and simmer for about 30 minutes. Cool slightly, then strain through a very fine sieve. Cool completely, refrigerate and use within 2 days, or freeze and keep for up to 3 months.

INDEX

READ MORE IN PENGUIN

In every corner of the world, on every subject under the sun, Penguin represents quality and variety – the very best in publishing today.

For complete information about books available from Penguin – including Puffins, Penguin Classics and Arkana – and how to order them, write to us at the appropriate address below. Please note that for copyright reasons the selection of books varies from country to country.

In the United Kingdom: Please write to *Dept. EP, Penguin Books Ltd, Bath Road, Harmondsworth, West Drayton, Middlesex UB7 ODA*

In the United States: Please write to *Consumer Sales, Penguin USA, P.O. Box 999, Dept. 17109, Bergenfield, New Jersey 07621-0120.* VISA and MasterCard holders call 1-800-253-6476 to order Penguin titles

In Canada: Please write to *Penguin Books Canada Ltd, 10 Alcorn Avenue, Suite 300, Toronto, Ontario M4V 3B2*

In Australia: Please write to *Penguin Books Australia Ltd, P.O. Box 257, Ringwood, Victoria 3134*

In New Zealand: Please write to *Penguin Books (NZ) Ltd, Private Bag 102902, North Shore Mail Centre, Auckland 10*

In India: Please write to *Penguin Books India Pvt Ltd, 706 Eros Apartments, 56 Nehru Place, New Delhi 110 019*

In the Netherlands: Please write to *Penguin Books Netherlands bv, Postbus 3507, NL-1001 AH Amsterdam*

In Germany: Please write to *Penguin Books Deutschland GmbH, Metzlerstrasse 26, 60594 Frankfurt am Main*

In Spain: Please write to *Penguin Books S. A., Bravo Murillo 19, 1° B, 28015 Madrid*

In Italy: Please write to *Penguin Italia s.r.l., Via Felice Casati 20, I–20124 Milano*

In France: Please write to *Penguin France S. A., 17 rue Lejeune, F–31000 Toulouse*

In Japan: Please write to *Penguin Books Japan, Ishikiribashi Building, 2–5–4, Suido, Bunkyo-ku, Tokyo 112*

In South Africa: Please write to *Longman Penguin Southern Africa (Pty) Ltd, Private Bag X08, Bertsham 2013*

READ MORE IN PENGUIN

A SELECTION OF FOOD AND COOKERY BOOKS

Traditional Jamaican Cookery Norma Benghiat

Reflecting Arawak, Spanish, African, Jewish, English, French, East Indian and Chinese influences, the exciting recipes in this definitive book range from the lavish eating of the old plantocracy to the imaginative and ingenious dishes of slaves and peasants.

The 30-Minute Cook Nigel Slater

'The whiff of kaffir lime leaves, cumin and ginger wafts from the pages . . . Slater is a very relaxed and relaxing kitchen companion – and I can think of no one more likely to coax timid cooks into a spirit of culinary adventure' – *Financial Times*

From Anna's Kitchen Anna Thomas

Anna Thomas, whose classic book *The Vegetarian Epicure* has long been a bestseller, has now put together over sixty mouth-watering vegetarian menus. From simple suppers to festive dishes, there is something for everyone, all year round, in Anna's kitchen.

Jane Grigson's Fish Book Jane Grigson

A new edition of Jane Grigson's imaginative and comprehensive guide to the delights of cooking and eating fish. 'A splendid book . . . Most Britishers are rather shy of fish and how to cook it . . . This book will change all that' – *Evening Standard*

Flavours of Greece Rosemary Barron

From the sharp olives, the salty feta and the delicate seafood of the first courses to the fragrant honey pastries and luscious figs of the desserts, Greek food offers a feast of variety that changes with the seasons. With wit and enthusiasm Rosemary Barron shows us how to recreate them in our own kitchen, for family meals or when entertaining.

BY THE SAME AUTHOR

Floyd on Oz

Join celebrated supercook Keith Floyd on the trip of a lifetime down under. Against a background of lively anecdotes and vivid impressions of people and places, he takes us on a culinary extravaganza, re-creating the versatility and deliciousness of Australian cookery. Beginning in Sydney, where he conjures up a seafood chowder while standing knee-deep in Watsons Bay, his journeys take him all over Australia from the major cities to the bush outback, from tropical rainforest to remote areas of desert. Wherever he goes he sets up his all-purpose stove or even occasionally cooks on the engine of his jeep.

'*Floyd on Oz* is written in snappy, amusing diary form so that it can be easily digested while the butter-crust trout tartlets are baking or the honey ice-cream is setting' – *Time Out*

Floyd on Spain

Keith Floyd ventures beyond the paella to discover the rich diversity of Spanish cuisine, one of Europe's best-kept culinary secrets. His journey through the tapas bars, restaurants and family tables of Spain, as seen in the television series, reveals the strong regional nature of Spanish food, resulting in an extraordinary variety of delicate soups, spicy stews, succulent roasts and delicious desserts. Whether cooking for a marquis in Toledo or celebrating the joys of eating with a working men's club in the Basque country, the inimitable Floyd captures the essential flavour of Spain.

'The recipes in *Floyd on Spain* are wonderful. The smells of herbs and onions, tomato sauce and grilled fish rise from the page and you want to get out, buy a hunk of hake and cook it with potatoes and garlic' – Prue Leith in the *Sunday Express*

BY THE SAME AUTHOR

Floyd on Italy

Travelling around Italy in search of authentic local dishes, Keith Floyd has brought his own inimitable style and expertise to recipes, interspersed with lively anecdotes. Simple dishes of antipasti range from toasted bread soaked in garlic and olive oil, to lightly grilled vegetables and potent, aromatic dips. For main meals there are traditional favourites such as saltimbocca as well as less well-known dishes such as white bean goulash and red mullet with pesto.

Far Flung Floyd

Keith Floyd's latest culinary odyssey takes him to the far flung East and the exotic flavours of Malaysia, Hong Kong, Vietnam and Thailand. Travelling by elephant, boat and trishaw, to say nothing of the occasional champagne-stocked limo, he explores the subtle and distinctive art of each South-east Asian cuisine, from Malaysian classics Satay and Beef Rendang to Vietnamese Spicy and Sour Prawn Soup and the awesomely hot Dynamite Drunken Beef from Thailand.

'The recipes in *Floyd on Italy* and *Far Flung Floyd* are terrific, as digestible and inviting as the author's talking versions' – Brigid Callaghan in *The Times*

forthcoming:

Floyd on Africa

Keith Floyd's wonderfully observant chronicle of cooking, eating and travelling in Zambia, Zimbabwe, Madagascar, South Africa and Lesotho is part safari and part recipe book. In his characteristically flamboyant fashion he describes the joys and the difficulties of creating delicious, inventive meals from the local produce. Inspired by the luscious tropical fruits in the markets, the plump fish from sparkling lakes and the game from the bush, he conjures up some unforgettable meals. Along the way he has many adventures, and, in his best ever cooking sketch, cooks bacon and eggs in the hot-box engine of a steam train.